Praise for *The Love Never Ends*

"An important book with valuable knowledge for those trying to understand their gift or wanting to know if their loved ones are still around them. Sunny is a vibrant, beautiful, and caring soul and a great teacher to many!"
—Lisa Williams, psychic medium
and best-selling author of *Survival of the Soul*

"Those unfamiliar with death and the dying process will find Johnston's approach fresh and new. She takes the reader by the hand and explains, through her own experiences and stories of her clients, that the afterlife really does exist and our soul continues to be connected to those we love. This book is a soothing balm for those who are grieving the loss of a loved one."
—Arielle Ford, author of *The Soulmate Secret*

"Sunny has written a book that fully explains death and the work of a psychic medium more than any book I have read. She comes from a place of knowing, using first-hand experience to paint a full and beautiful picture of this process."
—Madisyn Taylor, cofounder
and editor in chief of DailyOM

"In her new book *The Love Never Ends*, spiritual facilitator Sunny Dawn Johnston beautifully and skillfully draws upon her personal experiences, and those of her clients, students, and audience members, to give new meaning to death. This easy-to-read collection opens the door to redefining your deepest beliefs of love and death, and sheds new light on what each day of our lives can mean. I love this book!"

—Gregg Braden, *New York Times* best-selling author of *The Turning Point, The Divine Matrix,* and *The God Code*

"A voice of compassion gives us the strength to let go of our fear, and the voice of love gives us the inspiration to live and heal. Sunny Dawn Johnston's voice is an expression of both compassion and love as she guides us through the path of healing and understanding so that our heart can blossom with love again."

—don Miguel Ruiz Jr., author of *The Five Levels of Attachment*

"Sunny Dawn Johnston's compassionate heart and gifted way of teaching is inspiring; we recognize her experience as our own, leading us to our loved ones and our true essence. Sunny's earnest spirit injects us with the joy of knowing we are never alone."

—Peggy Rometo, intuitive healer, psychic medium, and author of *The Little Book of Big Promises*

"Sunny Dawn Johnston brings a real and tangible connection between the worlds, not only as a true example of her wisdom but as a transparent and loving way-shower in *The Love Never Ends.*"

—Simran Singh, founder of 11:11 Media and author of *Conversations with the Universe* and *Your Journey to Enlightenment*

"Sunny is an absolute angel in the lives of many, including my own. In her transformational new book, she leads you on a journey that will make you question what you think you know about life after death. This is a must-read for those ready to expand beyond their fears of death and understand the true nature of the infinite soul."

—Cari Murphy, international best-selling author,
award-winning media host, and Soul Success coach

"In her compassionate and caring work as an angel communicator and medium, Sunny Dawn Johnston has helped thousands overcome their fear of death or losing a loved one. Her book is a personal and transformational work that gives you a glimpse into her reality where there is no loss, no real 'death' of the soul, and indeed only love. If you have fears about the 'end' of life, read this book and set your soul free!"

—Ann Albers, author,
angel communicator, and modern mystic

"*The Love Never Ends: Messages from the Other Side* is a resonant treasure trove of stories and teachings that share the healing power of love, directly from the heart and soul of the inspired Sunny Dawn Johnston. Whether our loved ones are still with us or have passed over, *The Love Never Ends* shows us that we are eternally connected to those we deeply care for, and there is nothing to fear in life nor death. Truly, there is only love."

—Heather McCloskey Beck , author of *Take the Leap*

"*The Love Never Ends* is a must-read for anyone who has faced the loss of a loved one. Through her own personal story as well as those of her clients Sunny Dawn Johnston gives us validation that life goes on. More importantly, her message rings loud and clear: Love will prevail!"

—Dr. Steven Farmer, author of *Earth Magic*
and *Healing Ancestral Karma*

Sunny Dawn Johnston

The LOVE
NEVER
ENDS

Messages *from* the
OTHER SIDE

Hier◉phant publishing

Cover design by Adrian Morgan
Cover and author photos by Kris Voelker
Interior design by Jane Hagaman

Hierophant Publishing
8301 Broadway, Suite 219
San Antonio, TX 78209
888-800-4240
www.hierophantpublishing.com

If you are unable to order this book from your local bookseller, you may order directly from the publisher.

Library of Congress Control Number: 2014911453

ISBN 978-1-938289-35-4

10 9 8 7 6 5 4 3 2 1

Printed on acid-free paper in the United States of America

This book is dedicated to
LOVE . . .
in any and all forms it arrives in!

Every exit is an entry to somewhere else.

—Tom Stoppard

Contents

Preface

The Spirit World Speaks

The best and most beautiful things in this world cannot be
seen or even heard, but must be felt with the heart.
—Helen Keller

I began having conscious experiences with the spirit world as
a young teenager. I had felt the presence of spirits for many
years, but I was not really aware of what I was feeling and didn't
really understand it. The experiences were infrequent; I knew
I felt a presence, but beyond that I didn't have a clue.

One of the first experiences I can remember with the spirit
world was at age thirteen. I awoke at one in the morning to a
brilliant, glowing being hovering above my bed. But I wasn't
afraid, because the peaceful energy that emanated from this
glow felt like pure love. I soaked it up and felt calm and supported as I drifted back to sleep.

When I woke in the morning, I thought to myself, "OK, that
was not normal. What could that have been?" I went downstairs
and told my mom about the experience, and she told me that
it was my guardian angel. It made sense to me, even though I
had never even thought about having a guardian angel. It just
felt right. She also went on to share with me that earlier that
night she had come into my room and prayed over me. She

had asked God and the angels to surround me and protect me, as she had been worried about my emotional state. Once she said that, I realized that I had awakened to the manifestation of her prayers. This experience opened my eyes and piqued my curiosity. I wanted to know more, to experience more. I wanted to feel that serenity and unconditional love again.

It was shortly after that experience that the Lady on the Stairs showed up in my house. She would turn the TV on and off, change the radio station to a song I was thinking about, and pop movies in and out of the VCR. I thought I was nuts. I had felt her spirit since we had moved into the house earlier that year. There was a presence. I didn't know what else to call it or how else to describe it. At first it kind of freaked me out, so I didn't talk about it. And no one else talked about it either, which is why I really did think I was crazy. But then my little brother, five years old at the time, told me about the Lady on the Stairs. Although he was eight years younger than I was, I knew he was telling me this so that it would validate my intuition.

When I finally asked my mom about this Lady on the Stairs, she said she believed that the lady I described was the woman who lived in the house many years ago, when it was first built. Although she did not die in the house, she loved that home. It was love that called her back, and it was the memories of love that caused her to choose to spend her time there. Not all of her time, but certainly enough time that we named her the Lady on the Stairs. She was never scary to us, but to others, well, let's just say the hair on the back of their necks would raise for some unknown reason as they ran up the stairs. We always knew the reason—it was the Lady.

This type of thing became "normal" in my house, and it began to shift the self-judgment I had about my intuition. My mother was a wonderful channel of spirit, and she taught us that this "weird stuff" was real. She encouraged me to learn more and to meet with some of her astrology and psychic friends, and I did. I went to hypnotherapy sessions, crystal healings, and past-life regressions. It was a whole new world, one I embraced when no one my age was looking. My mom told me I could ask questions to the spirit world, and get answers. . . . And I did.

If it weren't for my little brother and his gift of clairvoyance and my mother and her validation that the spirit world was real, I never would have trusted my intuition enough to believe that what I was feeling in that little corner of the stairs was real. I see now that this experience was the beginning of my awareness of life after death. I believe it set me on the path that would become my destiny. Thirty years later, I serve as a bridge between the two worlds, offering validation that not only does the spirit world exist, but that the soul is eternal and love never ends.

I have found that many people struggle to trust their intuition, many for the same reasons that I did. Some were never taught about intuition, or the spirit world, so they just didn't know. Others were scared or taught that it was bad or evil. If you are finding yourself in this same funky place right now— knowing you have gifts, but not owning them, or letting fear hold you back—take a class, read a book (this one is a great choice), or attend a seminar. Jump in with both feet and learn whatever you can so that you can understand and develop your connection with the spirit world. It is so important!

Introduction

Death is just birth in disguise.
—Annie Kagan, *The Afterlife of Billy Fingers*

Perhaps you're reading this book because you've recently lost a loved one and are grieving, and you're wondering how you'll fill the void they've left with their passing. Maybe you want to communicate with them and are looking for some ways to spot if they're trying to get in touch with you. Or maybe you're trying to get in touch with a loved one who passed a while back, and you've been thinking about them a lot recently.

If you're in the very difficult position of anticipating a loved one's imminent passing—perhaps someone close to you is facing a terminal illness, and you're seeking knowledge and comfort about what is in store for them on the other side—I feel strongly you will find hope in the pages that follow.

Or perhaps you are someone who's aware of your own psychic abilities already, and you're looking to enhance those skills by learning to communicate with those who've moved on. In order to better serve you (and your clients), you'll want to know about effective communication with the other side, and how to convey that to others.

And lastly, perhaps you are someone who wants to understand more about this enigmatic, unavoidable topic of death and the afterlife.

If any of the situations above apply in your life, then this book is for you.

Finding the gift in death is not easy. I have lost three dear friends to suicide over the past five years, and yet even amidst the finger-pointing and blame I found love. I have had three miscarriages, and the pain and loss I experienced have turned into gratitude for the love and support I have from my babies in the spirit world. My grandmother's tragic death came too soon, and even in her passing I found love. I have lost many clients and students over the years to heart disease, accidents, cancer, murder, overdoses, and everything in between. And the one constant I always see—without exception—is love.

I tell you this not to emphasize how hard my life's been, or to suggest that you must endure the pain of losing many loved ones in order to fully understand death. Rather, I hope that by sharing my stories and experience they will help ease the fear and anxiety of death. Death in my life has been a gift, even when I didn't know it. Luckily, with the help of my angels and deceased loved ones, I have learned to find the gift. Even in the deep, deep sadness it is possible to find the gift, to find the love. I'll show you some examples of this from my life, but more importantly, I'll show you how to apply this knowledge to find the love in your own life as well.

I believe we are here, on this physical planet, to love and to be loved. Period. When our physical body dies, the love lives on, not only in the memories we have of our dearly departed, but in our day-to-day experiences with their spirits. The love that they have for us is evident in our everyday life, if we can just learn their new language.

1
Our Fear of Death

• •

Perhaps they are not stars, but rather openings in heaven
where the love of our lost ones pours through and shines
down upon us to let us know they are happy.

—Inuit saying

For a lot of us, the word "death" conjures up one idea pretty
consistently: fear. Fear of the unknown. Fear of losing all of our
loved ones. Fear of dying and leaving our loved ones behind.
Fear of what happens when we die. There are so many fears
around death that they actually have a term for it: death anxiety.

Instinctually, we are afraid of anything that is unknown.
As we are growing up, this instinct is affirmed by our family,
friends, religious groups, schools, and communities, to name
a few. Fear of the unknown, and a general tendency to distrust
anything outside the norm, in many ways helps mold societies.
This isn't necessarily healthy, and it can actually strengthen the
fear beyond its natural scope.

Death, I think it's safe to say, is *the* greatest unknown in
our physical world. While there are near-death experiences
(NDEs) and mediumship experiences that tell us some of the
story, we're still left with a good bit of uncertainty and wanting
real proof of what happens after we die.

Death is a seemingly permanent thing to many. Life, on the other hand, is something we experience every day; it is constant, and yet also always evolving. Life is also fragile: We're here one moment and gone the next. So we grasp the fragile, familiar thing and avoid the permanent, unknown one.

For most people, the absolute answer to releasing the fear of death comes when there is complete conviction that life never ends, that it is eternal: no beginning called birth or ending called death. This is the only reason I no longer fear death, and I have to tell you, you must have an experience that proves it to you beyond a shadow of a doubt. I have had these experiences over and over and over again. While I cannot recreate these experiences for you, I can share my stories in hopes that they will help.

They say a smart person learns from their mistakes; but a wise person learns from the mistakes (or experiences) of others. It is my intention that as I share my own personal stories and encounters with spirits on the other side, they will help you heal the fears you have about death. In doing so, this will allow you the opportunity to live a fear-free life. When we release the fear and heal, what we are left with is love . . . and in my experience, love never ends. Join me on this journey, and see for yourself.

Fear of Life

I think it's pretty well established that we live in a fear-ridden world. And while death is a very scary thing for many people, I want to begin with an even more dangerous type of fear: the fear of life.

The summer of my seventh grade year, my family and I went on vacation to Yellowstone National Park in Wyoming. The park was beautiful. We saw Old Faithful, the world's most recognizable geyser. It was one of the most captivating things my thirteen-year-old eyes had ever seen. It was gigantic, and I was in awe of its power. As I stood there and watched this force of nature erupt, I was amazed by its beauty—and at the same time disgusted by its rotten egg smell. I remember being shocked that something so beautiful could smell so terrible. I was experiencing complete contrast.

I had never really thought about my place in the world or my size in comparison to other things. But on this day, life changed for me. As I watched through my adolescent eyes, I felt as though I was a tiny, insignificant part of a massive world. I was haunted almost by the bigness of Old Faithful and the smallness of me. It was unsettling, and I tried to push the thoughts away. And I did a pretty good job . . . for a while.

That night, as I lay in my bunk in the camper, I couldn't keep my fearful thoughts away. We were camping at a small, isolated campground: no lights anywhere and pitch-black except for the stars and moonlight shining through the curtains right above my head. As I looked up into the night sky, thoughts of life and death overtook my mind. I imagined all kinds of stories about what could happen. A bear might come into the park and eat us. A murderer might be on the loose. I'd heard that mountain lions had attacked someone there recently. If it could happen to them, it could happen to me. All of these thoughts just brought more fear into my body as I lay there thinking. What happens when we die? What is God? Where is He? Why does almost everyone refer to God as a He? Why does God allow terrible things to happen to people? And why am I here? How on earth could I, little old me, be of any significance in this great big world?

I began thinking about all the things that happen in life and how scary it all was. As I looked at the stars, I was frozen in fear. I was trying to be quiet as my family was nearby, all sleeping in the camper as well. My tears turned into sobs as the questions of life and the possibilities of never having any answers sunk in, and I muffled my cries with my pillow. I was afraid. Of what exactly, I wasn't sure yet. What I do know is the fear was palpable.

I hadn't been raised with a particular religion, but I had been exposed to Mormonism, having grown up in Salt Lake City, Utah. Most of my exposure to religion was fear-based. In my experience there was judgment, condemnation, and a lot of rules that made it hard for me to feel good about myself. I grew up in a time and place where you weren't supposed to drink caffeine or alcohol, smoke cigarettes, or have sex before marriage. And if you did do any of these things, you were not worthy of God's love. In my thirteen-year-old mind and heart, I didn't understand. It seemed like the complete opposite of what I felt and believed in. I had an innate feeling that God (Spirit/Universe/Source/the Divine) was love. But most of what I'd learned about religion did not feel loving to me. When I thought about all the rules and the rights and wrongs, I felt like I could never live up to all of that. And those feelings had been validated throughout my life experiences. In truth, this life seemed much scarier than the afterlife.

After pondering my thoughts a bit, a feeling of knowing came over me, a deep knowing from within, that I was love. It moved through me like a chill, from one end of my body to the other. I felt calm enough then to finally fall asleep. I had found some peace, if only for a few hours. It had blown in like a gentle midnight breeze. I now know that the love I felt move through me that night was that of my angels, reminding me of who I really am.

Upon awaking the next day, although calm, I felt crazy. I was feeling complete contrast. I had this intense fear of not being good enough or worthy of love; and then I had this innate knowing that I *was* love. It made no sense. I was so confused and afraid. It wasn't the first time in my life that I had felt this contrast, for of course we all have contrast throughout life. But it may have been the first time I was truly conscious of it. I did not like it. I never wanted to feel the way I had felt that night. Ever again. I remember thinking, If there is a God, please don't ever let me feel this way again. I also asked myself, If God is a loving God, then why did all of these rules matter? If I am love, then how could there be anything wrong with me?

It was these questions and the varying answers from so many different people that would later call me to my life's work. The contrast between light and dark, fear and love, hope and pain, sadness and joy lived within me. Acknowledging that I carried these questions within myself, and then searching for the answers that felt true for me, would be my challenge over the next fifteen years.

Fear of Dying and the Unknown

I was raised in an environment that depicted death as scary, sad, and difficult. This view of death is common in our culture. While many people have an unsettling early memory of death, mine was extremely unusual.

When I was three years old we lived in the Philippines. It was Easter weekend, and I was sitting on my dad's 6'4" shoulders, towering over the entire crowd and unknowingly witnessing the sacred ritual of crucifixion that is part of their traditional Easter celebration. My father told me that the crucifixion was done to honor Christ and was a display of love, but I was too young to understand religion consciously and his explanation did nothing to calm me down. I watched in fear, terrified that they might do the same thing to me. Trembling, I climbed down my dad as quickly as I could and buried my face in his arms so that I did not have to watch it.

From that point, I never wanted to witness or experience anything associated with religion or death again. That's why I was initially what you might call a reluctant medium. As an adult, I was intrigued by the spirit world, and I loved being of service to others and helping them along their journey, but I was also scared. Not of the spirit world, though. It was the grief and mourning of death that was overwhelming and scary to me. The physical pain I felt in connection with how people died was overpowering, and the heaviness of it all was just too much for my sensitive soul. I was happy to do readings, happy to connect with the angels and teach people how to connect with theirs, but I drew the line at death. I didn't want any part of it, to the point of if I was doing a psychic reading and I saw or felt deceased energies around someone, I'd just ignore them. I did not want to do that part of it—and I didn't—until a little boy named Carl walked into my heart.

My First Experience Communicating with the Dead

Many years ago, I was doing readings at the Arizona State Fair. I had seen a lot of people over the week, and I still had ten days to go. It was late afternoon and the 100-degree heat was wearing on my sunny disposition. The other reader at my booth had just gone for the afternoon, leaving me there alone. I was secretly hoping no one else would come because I was tired and hot and hungry. So when the man wandering by asked me what I did, I answered him without even looking up. I told him I was doing readings. With my head still down, I stayed focused on my book and hoped he'd go away.

He grabbed the chair, however, turned it around backward so the back of it was up against my table, and sat down. I looked up, realizing that I wasn't being very present, and asked him his name. In a gruff voice that matched his weathered exterior the man introduced himself as Mike. I couldn't help but have compassion for him. He was a guy who looked like his life had been a long, hard road. I could tell he had suffered from addiction, although he felt pretty clear now. As I was just observing his energy, he asked me if we were going to get started, which kind of brought me out of my daze.

I asked him if he was open to saying a prayer together, which is something that at that point I didn't normally do. I thought it was odd, but Spirit knew what I was going to need, obviously. Mike agreed, and after a short prayer I went into the reading.

As I answered Mike's questions through my guidance, I kept feeling the presence of a little boy, about four years old. He had beautiful eyes and the sweetest little face, and he kept appearing over Mike's shoulder. I tried to ignore him and just forge on, because I really didn't want to do mediumship. But the little boy was persistent. Eventually, growing impatient, the little boy blurted out in a high-pitched voice, "Tell my dad I'm OK!"

Oh boy, here we go, I thought. I really didn't want to do this, but the little boy was so demanding and such a strong presence that I couldn't deny him anymore. So I took a breath and began to share.

"Mike, I have a little boy here. He stands over your left shoulder. He seems to be the age of four. He has dark eyes, straight sandy brown hair, and a beautiful smile. He tells me to tell you he is OK." As I said these words, which I could barely get out, this tough motorcycle man melted into tears. He put his head down and just cried. Then I cried too, as I could feel his sadness and absolute heartbreak.

As we both sat there in silence, the little boy, Carl (he shared his name with me nonverbally), began showing me what appeared to be a movie. I watched and listened with my whole body, tuning out the crowded fair and focusing only on him—a boy no one else could see. I saw this little boy with two men, walking in the desert. I watched in horror as this beautiful little boy, so full of life, was shot. I winced as I felt the pain in my own head and watched him fall to the dusty, cold desert ground. I was stunned. As I took a breath and tried to regain my composure, tears fell down my face and my body responded as if I had just witnessed this boy's murder firsthand.

I began shaking, and it was Carl's words again that called me back to the present moment. "It's not my dad's fault. Please tell him it is not his fault. I know he loves me. I see it every day. Please tell him to stop punishing himself." I sat there, stunned and unable to speak, hoping this was just my imagination. But as I looked up and into Mike's eyes, I knew the truth. This was his demon, the heaviness in his heart, the thing that haunted him night after night, day after day. He thought there was something that he could have done to prevent this.

As I took a breath, I realized that Mike knew what I was seeing. It was like he had tapped into my vision and watched it anew. He looked at me with that nod of "Ya, I know, it's hard to believe, isn't it?" He then waited for me to say something.

I didn't know where to start. What do you say? I had just witnessed the murder of a four-year-old . . . and the four-year-old is standing right in front of me with a smile on his face, happy as can be, just wanting to be seen and heard. I was totally unprepared.

Once my initial shock wore off, I shared these messages with Mike that Carl so desperately wanted him to hear: "There wasn't anything you could have done. It was all planned out. Nobody could have saved me. Thank you for getting sober. Let go of the anger toward her, it is making you sick. Love me enough to forgive yourself." And, most importantly, "I love you always and forever, and I am with you."

There were other things shared, but as of this writing the legal case is on appeal after twenty-three years. In the interest of the case I cannot discuss any more, but suffice it to say Carl shared graphic details of the days preceding his death and the death itself. He validated many of his father's beliefs but counseled him to let go of his rage. (I know, it sounds strange that a four-year-old can be a counselor; but remember, Carl isn't four anymore . . . he's in spirit and wiser than many.) Carl told us that he was with the angels, and as he began to drift away, I was left with the vision of that beautiful little smile, and a reminder from him: "I am good!"

When Mike finally got up to leave an hour later, I was still shaking and we were both crying. As he walked away, I couldn't stop thinking about my own four-year-old son at home. All I wanted to do was go home and hug my kids. The thought of what had happened to Carl nauseated me. I needed to throw up to get that feeling out of my body, which I did several times before leaving the fairgrounds.

As soon as I was alone in my car, I lost it. I called my mom on my drive home to have her help ground me, as I felt like I would just drift away. My head was fuzzy, and I wanted to check out of my body for a little while. Once I got home, I hugged my sons so tightly it hurt.

As I settled down a bit, I tried to imagine what my life would be like if I did mediumship like this every day. All I could hear was my head saying, *No way—this is exactly why you don't want to do this. It's just too intense and too painful.* That night I fell into a fitful sleep thinking about Carl and Mike.

I didn't sleep much for the next few weeks. I couldn't get Mike and Carl out of my head. It was so unfair. Why must an innocent child suffer such a tragic and painful death? But I understand now that things may seem unfair in this human realm because we don't see the bigger picture. It is hard to understand with our limited human perception, as we base things on good and bad, right and wrong. From all of my experiences with the spirit world, this one thing is true: Carl left in the perfect way for him and his legacy. Meaning, it was purposeful for his journey—and for Mike's journey and the others who loved him as well.

What I learned that day at the fair was that mediumship is not about fun and games. It is hard. It is painful. It is heartbreaking. And it is life-changing for everyone involved. I had both given and received a gift that day. Carl gave me a gift by coming to me and through me. This was just one of several deep spiritual experiences I'd had in my life.

The profound love and peace that he came to me with, such tremendous mercy and benevolence, were a gift I have never forgotten. Carl taught me that love is always the answer. Always. This kid scared the hell out of me and inspired me at the same time. His message of forgiveness to his dad touched me as well. What perceived wrongdoings in my life did I need to forgive and let go of to let love in? My challenges paled in comparison to Mike's. I had it easy.

Carl gave Mike a gift, too. A gift of knowing that love never ever ends. A validation of a truth that was buried within Mike's heart, unrecognizable until he heard the words he had dreamt of ever since that cold December day: *I love you and I always will.*

It was a reminder that his son was watching over him, loving him through it all. There was no blame, no hate or anger . . . only love. And love heals.

I was also able to give Carl a gift, by being the voice by which he could speak. I got out of the way enough to let Carl tell his dad how much he loved him and how proud he was that he had gotten sober. No easy task, especially for the father of a murdered son. Carl validated Mike's feelings and acknowledged the tremendous pain and anger he carried through thousands of sleepless nights.

I was a messenger—a messenger of love. I saw this as the greatest gift that could ever be given. There were times when I felt unworthy of it, as if I didn't deserve it. But I quickly got over that when I saw the faces of my clients light up at the mention of a name, or a scent of perfume that their loved one wore, or a story that validated the truth of their loved one's presence.

That day, that crazy little day at the fair, was a turning point for me; I could no longer go back to my somewhat "normal" life. If I could lift someone's pain and grief by offering some healing through the messages, if I could provide some sense of closure, if I could teach them how to communicate with their loved ones after they passed, if I could share the truth that love never ends that I had witnessed so many times in my life, if I could just get over the fear . . . then I could really make a difference in this world. And that I wanted to do! It was time to truly step into the work that Spirit had so ingeniously set me up for. It was time.

So, with that awareness, I stepped in big time! I saw clients for mediumship readings. I joined a not-for-profit organization, Find Me, and began donating my extra time working on missing persons cases. I spoke at events around the Phoenix

Valley on the subject, and I began to teach. I wanted people to know and understand that if they had a heart connection with someone in the spirit world, then they could in fact communicate with them. Of course, I could make that connection for them, but they too could learn the language. All one needed was to understand how it all worked, something I will share more about later in this book.

My First Experience
Helping Someone Cross Over

I've found that love shows up in a variety of ways—often in places we are not expecting, including the nonphysical. This was certainly the case during one of the most influential events in my life.

As you may know, I have done a lot of work with the archangels. (Much of this is explained in my first book, *Invoking the Archangels*.) But back in 1999, I was not as familiar with Archangel Uriel and his energy, even though I had read about him when I was a teenager. I had not had my own experience with him in a way that I could consciously remember at that point, but looking back now, I realize that many of my thoughts, ideas, and inspirations had been guided by the wise energy of Archangel Uriel for quite some time. Archangel Uriel is often referred to as the Angel of Illumination. He helps us see the bigger picture and often guides us with prophetic information. Being able to see the bigger picture while in the midst of a difficult situation can help you make decisions that are for the highest good for all involved. This was the case for me when my son's paternal grandmother, Delores, had a stroke.

It all began with a phone call from Crew's biological father, John. I hadn't talked to him for a couple years, so I was surprised when I heard from him. He told me that his mom had had a stroke. She had very little brain stem activity, was in a coma, and they were going to take her off life support. The doctors thought she would transition immediately after the life support was disconnected. My heart sank as I listened to John talk.

Delores, my former mother-in-law, and I had definitely had our ups and downs. But as the years went by, Delores and I had developed a strong relationship. Shortly before Delores left this physical world, she shared with me intimate details about her life, specifically her frustrations with herself as a mother and with her children. She wished she could have done some things differently. I tried to reassure her that we do the best we can with what we know and what we have to work with. She would usually just respond with a sigh. That was the Delores I knew and loved.

My heart was broken. I wanted to be there to tell her goodbye, but there was no time. As I sat on the floor teary-eyed, I felt a sense of sadness yet hopefulness. I can't explain it. I tried to finish feeding my youngest son Arizona his breakfast, but I couldn't focus. I turned on *Blue's Clues* for him and went in my room to meditate and pray. As I sat in my chair, I kept asking if Delores had passed. Because of our strong bond, I thought I would be able to feel her spirit leave this earthly plane. I really had no basis for that, because I'd never been with anyone as they passed before, but that is how I felt.

An hour later, I still had not heard from John, so I tried to call him. I couldn't reach anyone. At first, I was angry because I thought she had died and no one had called me. Then I was angry because I didn't feel anything when she passed away. I must not have been tuned in if I couldn't feel her leave.

Then a strong intuitive feeling came over me: Delores was waiting for me! At first it didn't make any sense; that thought went against everything the doctors and John had told me. But I just kept hearing inside my head: "She is waiting for me."

I finally reached someone at one of her sons' houses and asked if she had passed yet. He said no, she hadn't. I was confused. Why was no one answering at the care center then? He told me everyone had left.

"What do you mean everyone left? Why is no one there with her?"

His response shocked me even more. "She is already gone to us. It is just too hard to watch her go, so we came back to the house." I was stunned and angry, yet not surprised. I knew that her children had a fear of death, and I knew it was their way of dealing with the situation; but I was also devastated and upset that she was alone.

I hung up the phone and sat quietly for a minute. I knew I needed to do something, but I was not sure what to do. It was a six-hour drive, and the doctors had said that she could go any minute. I knew I'd never make it to California in time to be with her, so I let the questions go.

It was then that Archangel Uriel first appeared to me, and the answer was so clear: "Yes, go, Sunny. You will make it; she is waiting for you; you will make it."

I questioned the guidance for a brief moment, but I knew it was the right thing to do. So I asked my new neighbor if she would care for my twenty-month-old child and pick up my other son from school and watch them until my mom got there or my husband got home from work. And then I asked her if she'd tell my husband that I was on a plane to California, and I'd call him that night to explain everything. I am sure she thought I was crazy! Now, this was a big step for me, because I had never left my children with anyone but family; so to ask a neighbor, actually a complete stranger, was quite unlike me. However, Spirit told me that it would be OK.

I changed my clothes and got on a plane to California, then rented a car once we'd landed. I still had a nearly two-hour drive with no traffic. During the drive, I kept praying that Delores would wait for me. My angels kept reminding me, over and over again, that Spirit wouldn't have me go through all of this and not have her there waiting for me when I got there. I knew there was divine guidance directing my every move. But every once in a while, my ego would step in for a little visit and I'd freak out. So to calm myself, I turned on the radio. Sarah McLachlan's song "Angel" was playing. This made me cry. I felt as if it were validation that Delores would wait for me. A few minutes later, I changed the channel and the same song came on again. I was amazed. *OK*, I thought. *I get the message.*

Archangel Uriel was guiding me to her, and I would be there at the right time. Throughout the long drive, I changed the channel six more times and heard that song on every one. I was in awe of the power of the Universe as I realized that it was I who was in the arms of the angels, and they were guiding me to Delores.

Finally, I arrived. As I pulled into the parking lot, I took a deep breath, said a prayer to my guides and angels, and went in. I had never been around someone who was in a coma or about to die. I was worried that I might feel scared, but I felt calmer than I thought I would. A sense of peace filled my body as I walked into the room and saw Delores lying in bed. I was relieved to see her there, thankful that I had made it, and grateful that she was not going to die alone. It was so important to me to know that our love connection had allowed me to make it there and share this sacred time with her, in whatever form it would unfold.

The first thing I noticed was that Delores looked like she was sleeping. She didn't seem to be in any pain. I thanked her for waiting for me and told her I was there to be with her while she made her transition. Then I sat on the bed on her left side and just stopped and studied her for a few minutes.

After a few minutes I had to leave the room because my heart was full of emotion. I questioned what I was doing there, why I had come. My mind told me that I didn't know what to do in this situation and that it was going to be scary, but my heart told me to stay.

I called the house where Delores's children were staying to let them know that I was there. I said I had come to be with her while she passed. They told me I could come over to the house if I wanted to and get something to eat. I declined, saying I planned to stay until she passed away. As I went back into her room to sit with her, I felt grief-stricken and outraged that not one of Delores's children was here with her. My mind wondered about the pain she might be in, knowing that none of her children were here to support her.

Suddenly, I felt the presence of someone behind me. I turned around and saw John standing in the hallway, crying. I got up and hugged him for at least five minutes. In that embrace, I felt all of the sadness, hurt, and frustration he was experiencing. We continued to hold each other in silence. It was an interesting moment. The anger and frustration that I felt toward Delores's family members dissolved, and all that remained was compassion. I understood now how difficult this was for him, and I felt the fear of death that had taken him over. We walked down the hallway for a bit and did not say a word. As we neared the exit, I told John I would call when she had gone. We embraced one last time, and he thanked me. If only I could have shared with him then what

I was about to discover so clearly for myself shortly: that love never dies.

I climbed into Delores's bed and lay down next to her. I put ChapStick on her dry lips. I talked with her and actually felt her talking back to me. I hugged her and held her hand. I told her how much I loved her, how sorry I was that I had moved and taken her grandson Crew away from her. I shared with her how hard I had tried to be a good mom and how hard it had been to leave her son to make a better life. I shared everything, held nothing back. There were long periods of silence in which I just listened to her breathe. The nurse said that her breathing would change, and it did—it would be heavy, then light. She would rattle off and on, and then return to more steady breaths for a while. I finally fell asleep beside her. It was such an incredibly peaceful time.

I woke up about an hour later to the television coming on, and it startled me. I knew from all my metaphysical studies that when spirit people enter a room, electrical systems sometimes get wacky. I watched Delores's breathing, but nothing happened. I turned the television off, but about ten minutes later it came back on. I turned it off again. I began to talk to Delores and tell her that it was OK for her to go. She could leave anytime, and I was staying with her until she did. Each time the television came on, I thought it was a sign that she was ready to pass. This happened four or five times.

Finally, I called the nurse and asked if someone could come and check out the TV. Maybe it wasn't spiritual electricity; maybe it was simply some bad wiring. They sent in a repairman, and he checked out everything and said it was fine. But to be sure it didn't happen again, he unplugged the power cable from the wall. He assured me that would take care of it. Well, twenty minutes later, it happened again. I called the repairman back in, and we both watched in amazement as the television came on. How could it be? I decided this was a serious sign, and Delores's passing was getting closer.

At the same time, I felt the energy in the room change. I believe her spirit family members were coming and gathering around her. I couldn't see them, but I was getting chills and feeling the energy move around me. It was about eight in the morning. I got up and got ready quickly, as I knew she was about to leave. Delores's breathing grew slower and slower. The death rattle the nurse had talked about had finally begun.

Now I was scared. I knew I needed to release the fear and trust Spirit, but I wasn't sure how. I felt out of control because I didn't know what exactly was going to happen. I asked the nurse what would happen next, and she simply said that Delores's heart would stop, and there would be no more noise.

I held Delores's hand and waited. I asked the angels to surround us both. I asked for the strength to help me through this next step in our journey. I prayed for Delores's freedom from a physical body that had served her so well.

As I continued my prayers, I had my last conversation with Delores. I heard her voice very clearly say, "Sunny, put my eyebrows on. Don't you let me leave here without my eyebrows on." I thought I was going crazy. I didn't know how to put eyebrows on!

In my mind, I said back to Delores, "I don't even have an eyebrow pencil. I can't do it." She responded, "Yes, you can. Don't let me leave without my eyebrows."

I giggled a bit. She was in the midst of her transition and was concerned about her brows. I thought to myself, Spirit does have a sense of humor! So who was I to argue? If my last expression of love in this physical world involved giving Delores eyebrows, then I was going to do it. I searched my makeup bag, and the closest thing I could find was a reddish-brown lip liner. So, I sharpened it up and added reddish eyebrows to Delores's gray and clammy yet very peaceful face. As I did, I could feel her gratitude. It was palpable.

As I stayed in this moment, Delores's breathing got louder and even slower. I asked the nurse to stay in there with me for an added comfort. I sat back down next to Delores's bed and held her hands in mine. I closed my eyes, and I put my head down by her heart. A few moments later, I felt this powerful, enormous energy rush through my arms at the same time I felt Delores release her physical body. A white energy moved like a wave through my hands to the bottom of my feet all the way up to the top of my head and out my crown. My entire body started shaking for several minutes, and then as quick as it came it was gone—and so was Delores.

Her spirit left as quickly as the energy that had come in through my hands and left through my crown. I couldn't move. I was present to what had just happened and was in awe. I knew at that moment that something incredible had happened to me that day, but I didn't realize how life changing it would be. Delores and I had spent her last seventeen hours on this Earth together in that room. The doctors had said she would be gone in a matter of minutes after taking her off life support, but she stayed. I believe she waited for me. In that short while I felt so many emotions—honor, responsibility, absolute love.

The days following Delores's death were transformational. I felt like I *must* get on my journey. That it was time. I felt like I was being guided from above as well as from within. I know that Archangel Uriel had supported me through the entire forty-eight hours I had spent getting to Delores and being with her. I believe that Delores is now one of my spirit guides and that she has guided me, step-by-step, to the life that I now live.

She "forced" me to face my fears, own my gifts, and speak my truth, and I will be forever grateful to her for this.

One thing that I now know, which I think is important to mention here, is that when someone dies it is possible to feel their spirit move through you at their time of death—even if you are not physically with them. If I had not been with Delores at the time of her passing, I believe I still would have felt her leave this Earth. When you have a strong love connection and the physical presence leaves, many people feel them leave. Some are even awakened out of a deep sleep or see their loved one's spirit as they leave.

There is a greater purpose in the midst of chaos, heartache, life changes, and even death. The inspiration and guidance I have received from Delores following her death is one of the pivotal reasons I am doing the work I am called to do now. The validation I received from my angels and guides that day allowed me to be present for one of the most transformational moments of my life. Seeing, feeling, and knowing the presence of love and its never-ending connection have allowed a sense of peace as I walk through life. This connection can be yours, if you will release the fear.

Release Your Fears

I believe that we are often trained to be fearful by our society at large and are not trained to trust; therefore, fear feels more natural and can be stronger than love. Because death is the ultimate unknown while we are in our physical forms, it brings with it a variety of fearful emotions. No matter what the basis for our fears or the ways in which we react to them, these fears will only result in a lowering of our vibration and a shutting down of our natural connection to Spirit. The first step in reversing this natural tendency is to consciously begin to become aware—and accepting of—your particular types of fears. Whether you fear the physical sensations of the dying process, the actual existence or nonexistence of an afterlife, the absence of those who have passed before you, or any of the other possible questions that surround death, the reassurance I can offer you through my experiences again starts with the foundation of what I believe to be true: the love never ends.

Fear of the End

A big reason a lot of people are afraid of death is because we have been taught that it is the end of life.

I have had encounters with thousands of deceased energies, and I would say that there is *no evidence* that there is an end! Maybe it is the end of life as we know it, but this is not the end. It's not. It is a change—a change into a new form. You are eternal, as we all are, and death is as natural a thing as birth. Someone's death here on Earth is a birth and celebration in the afterlife. And when someone "dies" in the afterlife, it is a birth and celebration here.

I get very different answers from spirits about what's on the other side of this life. But I do know that life and love are infinite, and the afterlife is your creation. I have come to believe that we go where we believe we will go, and we create whatever it is we want to create. You are a vibrational, energetic being constantly creating and expanding—and that doesn't end when you leave this planet.

I believe that we go to the sprit world when we leave our bodies. Some people call this heaven. I do not necessarily believe in a so-called heaven or hell. However, to me the spirit world is what others would call heaven. They really feel like the same thing to me, just different words to describe the same place. So for this book, I will refer to them interchangeably.

There are varying degrees of heaven, based on vibration. Therefore, we go to the level that we vibrate to based on our thoughts, words, and actions when we were in physical form. Those who were in a high vibration in the physical realm will be in a higher vibration in the spirit realm. Those who were in a lower vibration in the physical realm will be in a lower vibration in the spirit realm as well. Simply said, we will hang with the energies of those that are on the same level of spiritual evolution as we are.

What does heaven look like? Heaven looks like whatever you want it to look like, because it is based on your thoughts. I see heaven as being similar to our physical Earth, but with much brighter light and more intense colors and sounds; colors and sounds that cannot be explained in words.

Fear of Pain

Does dying hurt? A lot of us are scared to find out the answer to this question. The reality is that the way we leave this physical existence can be traumatizing and painful to the physical shell, but it doesn't necessarily have to be. While we might all hope to pass peacefully in our sleep one night, the reality is that not everyone does, and that can be scary.

The feedback I get from the spirit world is that during the dying process, the person's spirit is going in and out of his or her body. So, if you are with someone who's passing over and they seem to not be there, it's because oftentimes they aren't.

When someone's last breaths appear labored, it is hard to witness. When the breathing becomes very labored, it is often referred to as a "death rattle." The death rattle can be very difficult for those watching the transitioning of their loved ones. It may help you to know that by the time a person is in the final throes of the dying process and experiencing the death rattle, though it looks and sounds quite heinous, the person is unconscious and unaware of the discomfort because their spirit is no longer embodied, but more likely witnessing the events from above. Something you can do during the death rattle that might help comfort everyone is to hold your loved one's hands and get in sync with his or her breath, breathing opposite them, until you become one breath. We are one breath prior to birth, and we can become one breath during death as well. I was taught this technique, the Infinity Breath, in hospice training with Dannion Brinkley. It has been a fabulous technique to use when someone is transitioning.

If we are lucky, death can be as simple as just taking a breath. The spirit world has told me that dying feels a lot like going to sleep. Some spiritual teachers even suggest that we "die" every night when we leave our bodies for the dream state. The spirit can actually come and go throughout our lives—visit the other side, check out when we are in pain—but when the heart quits beating, the spirit has gone home.

Fear of Being Alone

As human beings, we have lived our life looking for that unconditional love and support that we know instinctively is part of the oneness we share in Spirit. We are a community of physical beings striving to strengthen that spiritual bond within ourselves as well as with everyone else on this physical journey. It is certainly understandable, then, that one of our greatest fears associated with death would be the fear of ultimately being alone.

Even if you are seemingly alone in the physical world, know that you truly aren't alone. You have your guardian angels and spirit guides right beside you, just like you did during your birth. They are beside you throughout your entire journey. As you transition, your deceased loved ones, animals, friends, and other light beings are also there with you. So no, you do not die alone.

After we have passed on, there is a life review. This is where you witness everything that happened in your life . . . every feeling, every emotion, and every experience. Every person whose life you've touched, and who's touched yours; every experience that you imparted to another being, both positive and negative. It is as if your story is played out on a movie screen. I've been told you can even fast-forward and rewind through different parts of it. You can also see how things might have turned out had you gone down a different road or made a different choice.

It is my understanding that one road isn't better than any other. They generally all wind up going to the same place. It is really just more about the experience and the expansion of you and, of course, your soul. As you go through this life review, there is no judge and jury. There is no one to judge or condemn you. It is an opportunity to study the life you lived and learn and grow from it with a new and different perspective. Because you are now in spirit, you can see from a higher vibration, and you can observe what each experience was truly about.

We can look forward to receiving the answers and understanding to the questions we asked while living at some point after we die, but the answers aren't always immediate.

As with any new experience in our lives, an opportunity for increased awareness and understanding is available to us if we are first open to these unfamiliar possibilities and perceptions. Our tendency to resist the new and unknown is often a protection mechanism or simply a matter of unconsciously adhering to previous belief systems without taking the time to evaluate these prospects for growth. By embracing the events that have been a part of my journey and allowing the insights and connections from the spirit world to become a guide to me, I have been able to overcome my initial reluctance and develop a valuable spiritual support system. This is absolutely possible for you too. Begin by acknowledging your initial fears, staying open to new perceptions, and allowing your vibration to raise as you release those fears. The payoff will be a connection to the spirit world that you may have never imagined!

2
Understanding Your Support System

Unconditional Love and Our Spiritual Helpers

● ●

Love is what we were born with. Fear is what we have
learned here. The spiritual journey is the relinquishment—
or unlearning—of fear and the acceptance of love back in
our hearts. Love is the essential existential fact. It is our ultimate reality and our purpose on earth. To be consciously
aware of it, to experience love in ourselves and others, is
the meaning of life.

Meaning doesn't lie in things. Meaning lies in us.
        —Marianne Williamson, *A Return to Love*

Love is much easier to experience than it is to define. Love is
a force of nature bigger than all of us, an energy that moves
through us all. It is a connection shared with another. It is the
light within us. It is our heart connection. And it never dies. No
matter how much our pain may trick us into thinking we want
to, we cannot control, demand, or dissipate love any more than
we can control the sun rising each morning. Love lives on in our
hearts, our memories, our stories, and, yes, our connections.

The first step in accepting this love from others is being able to love ourselves. For some of us, this isn't an issue. But my experience has taught me that many of us struggle with this. Let's take a minute to find out why and what to do about it.

Unconditional Self-Love

We all want to feel love. We hope for it, search for it, dream about it, and feel incomplete without it. It took me a while to love myself. Despite having a loving family, and a couple of friends, I was still searching for that feeling of complete and total love. As that young, insecure girl in Yellowstone National Park, I was longing to feel it.

In my journey to discover this kind of whole love, I began to look for it in the eyes of teenage boys. I begged for it through my good grades, my physical illnesses, and my strong work ethic. During those times, I didn't realize that I needed to discover it within before I would ever receive it from the outside world. Back then it was the outside world that I cared about. It was the acceptance of others that I was seeking, and it was the absolute knowing of my value that I could never quite reach. I knew somehow, somewhere, deep down inside that I was special. I knew that I was deeply loved and adored. I knew it at the core of my being, but all I saw in this physical world was that I was different—and different did not equal special (at least not in my book, anyway, and certainly not in any of the people's books that I cared to read). I could acknowledge that I was different, even that I was part of a different type of family, but I wanted to know how truly special I was.

I mention the importance of self-love here because after the death of a loved one, many people experience grief, anger, and emptiness, and they often feel disconnected from life. And there's only one kind of love that can fill us up, make us whole, and lift us up through the most difficult of times: unconditional self-love. If you don't have this, you could find yourself internalizing your feelings and perhaps making unhealthy choices because of your pain.

It may take some soul-searching, but discovering this unconditional self-love can allow us to see the greater vision around the loss of our loved ones, which ultimately can help us to connect with love again in the physical world. Our unconditional love of self is what calls us to stay present, to show up. When we show up for ourselves, when we are loving and kind to ourselves, we can feel the connection to our dearly departed loved ones much more strongly and deeply. Loving ourselves unconditionally allows us to be fully present in all experiences and allows us to walk the journey in a way that is honoring of ourselves and those we love. It is of absolute importance to the healing process.

True unconditional love is affection without any limitations. It does not come with conditions, stipulations, addendums, or codes. Love is not seeing experiences, situations, or people as good or bad, but simply as experiences. It's our perception of good and bad that colors our existence and how we feel about our life and the people we love and share life with. What's good for us may be bad for someone else. And what's bad for us may be good for someone else. What we saw as a sad time many years ago we may now see as one of our greatest blessings. The challenge and the gift in life are to see the blessings as they are happening and not have to wait years to spot the beauty of our experiences. It is all of these experiences, the perceived "good" and "bad," which make up this amazing life we live.

Spiritual Love

Spiritual love lives on from form to form as we move in and out of the physical body from lifetime to lifetime. This love recognizes the divine light in everyone and everything. This love is never-ending. It simply is. And it operates at different vibrational levels, as we'll see next.

The Vibrational Levels of the Spirit World

Everything created is energy, and energy vibrates at different levels. Just as a singer has a vocal range of notes she can sing, human beings have a vibrational range. In other words, you move up and down a vibrational scale. The more you work on loving yourself, the higher your vibration rises, and the easier it is to connect with higher vibrational beings. These higher vibrational beings can be your spiritual helpers, or as they might also be known as deceased loved ones, spirit guides, ascended masters, angels, or archangels. While we may be born on different places on the vibrational scale, we all possess the ability to reach the highest level through appreciation, forgiveness, joy, meditation, and love. If you wish to connect to higher vibrational beings, then you simply raise your own personal vibration.

You might be wondering why *you* need to raise *your* vibration. The universal Law of Attraction states that like energy attracts like energy, and because the beings in the spiritual realm do not like to lower their vibration, therefore you must raise yours to connect with them. The more you stay in a higher, lighter, clearer vibration, the more you will connect with the spiritual realm.

I have included here a diagram of the energetic vibrational scale. This will give you an idea of the vibrational ranges of spiritual helpers as I have come to experience and understand them. Each level is not good or bad; it just simply is.

Energetic Vibrational Scale

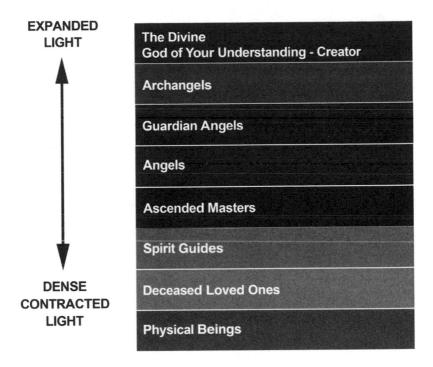

EXPANDED LIGHT

The Divine
God of Your Understanding - Creator

Archangels

Guardian Angels

Angels

Ascended Masters

Spirit Guides

DENSE CONTRACTED LIGHT

Deceased Loved Ones

Physical Beings

Let's begin with where we are, at the lowest level of vibration. **Physical beings** are you and me and everyone you see with a body and a heartbeat. While we are able to raise our vibration temporarily in order to communicate with those on the higher planes, we aren't able to sustain this permanently and must come back down after a while. The only way to ascend to a permanently higher vibration is through death.

Deceased loved ones are family, friends, coworkers, and loved ones who have passed. They have released the dense energy of their physical bodies and automatically moved up the vibrational scale. In my experience, there is often an amount of divine time, not measured time, when deceased loved ones can "prepare" to become spirit guides if they so choose. This is not typically an instantaneous move up the vibrational scale.

Spirit guides once inhabited a physical form and had the same journey or purpose as the physical beings they are now guiding. Upon leaving their physical bodies, spirit guides choose to become teachers or guides to those of us still in the physical realm. They offer guidance, comfort, and, at times, warnings and protection. Spirit guides are often the spiritual essence of deceased loved ones. They can guide multiple people, but they do not become angels. Humans that have transitioned can become only a guardian or a spirit guide. Angels are a high vibrational being that doesn't incarnate into a physical body, and a physical body doesn't become an angel. However, all humans already have guardian angels that guide and support them throughout their evolution.

Spirit guides can visit multiple people all at the same time. I have had that happen in my own family. Three different people, in different states, saw signs of my grandfather at almost the same time after he passed. Remember, a spirit guide doesn't have a body any longer, so it is not limited to being in one place at a time. A spirit guide is energy and can be everywhere and anywhere, all at once.

Moving further up the scale, the **ascended masters** are divine beings that lived earthly lives as great teachers, healers, or way-showers of ascension, such as Buddha and Jesus. Ascended masters come from all cultures modern and ancient, and they are often spoken of and remembered in a religious context. They released all their fears and grew and raised their vibrations in order to ascend, and they bring light and love to everyone regardless of their religious beliefs or feelings of worthiness. They teach that we are all worthy of love and guidance.

Angels, guardian angels, and archangels are higher vibrational beings that exist only in the spiritual realm and do not incarnate into physical form as humans and animals do. **Angels** help, guide, comfort, and assist us in our earthly journey by uplifting and protecting us. Each physical being is supported by one **guardian angel** throughout his/her entire physical life from birth until death. A guardian angel's job is to unconditionally love and protect us. **Archangels** are the powerful overseers of the angelic realm. Call on the archangels anytime for anything, and they will be there immediately.

Seven Archangels
You Might Call On for Help

Archangel Michael

Michael is the archangel of protection, guidance, and strength. When I call on his help, I visualize myself surrounded by a protective blue bubble. Michael helps with protection, direction, self-esteem, motivation, courage, commitment, faith, energy, vitality, life's purpose, and releasing fear.

Archangel Jophiel

Jophiel is the archangel of creativity, beauty, and art. When I call on Jophiel for help, I visualize a golden yellow light entering the top of my head and moving down my entire body. Jophiel helps with manifesting more beauty in your life through your thoughts and by supporting artists and artistic projects, interior design and decorating, releasing prejudice and ignorance, awakening, self-awareness, inspiration, hope, and joy. He helps those who feel spiritually lost, depressed, or in despair.

Archangel Chamuel

Chamuel is the archangel of unconditional love and adoration. As I invoke Archangel Chamuel, I imagine a vibrant pink energy surrounding my entire physical being. Chamuel helps with career, life purpose, finding lost items, building and strengthening relationships, world peace, and seeking soul mates.

Archangel Gabriel

Gabriel is the archangel of communication and is also known as the Messenger Angel. As I invoke Archangel Gabriel's energy, I visualize the white light of Gabriel coming down from the heavens and entering my body through my head, concentrating on my throat area. Gabriel helps with communication in any area, TV and radio work, adoption, child conception and fertility, and journalism and writing.

Archangel Raphael

Raphael is the archangel of healing. Raphael heals physical bodies as well as mental, emotional, and spiritual bodies. As I invoke Archangel Raphael's energy, I see emerald green energy completely surrounding my body with a healing presence. Raphael helps with eliminating or reducing addictions and cravings, healing on all levels, guidance and support for healers, physical and spiritual eyesight, clairvoyance, and finding lost pets.

Archangel Uriel

Uriel is the archangel that illuminates situations, gives prophetic information, and offers transmutation. As I invoke Archangel Uriel's energy of wisdom, I imagine myself completely enveloped in the color red, which guides me through my challenges. Uriel helps with insight, clarity, peace, vision, problem solving, writing, new ideas, study, and tests.

Archangel Zadkiel

Zadkiel is the archangel of forgiveness, mercy, and benevolence. As I invoke Archangel Zadkiel, I visualize a violet flame just above my head burning away the negative thoughts and feelings that hold me back from forgiving myself and others. Zadkiel helps with forgiveness of self and others, emotional healing, compassion, freedom, finding lost objects, and memory.

Throughout my life, angelic beings have presented themselves in all sorts of shapes, sizes, and forms, often determined by what I was feeling, seeing, or knowing in the moment. Their forms have changed and evolved over time as I've grown spiritually. Therefore, the definition or visual representation of angels can be as different as seashells on a beach. Each individual will experience angels based upon his or her own perceptions, and I believe that all impressions of the angelic realm are valid. Angels show themselves in a way that you are able to perceive and understand and are often gentle and comforting in their approach.

Finally, the **Divine** is the God of your understanding. My understanding of God does not come from religious beliefs or scripture, but rather from my own journey inward. When I reached a point in my life where I recognized I had to take responsibility for myself and that I had no control over anything or anyone but myself, I came to understand that God was in everyone and everything. I realized that God is *love.* I am God, you are God, and we are God, as are the wind, the trees, the oceans, the animals, the clouds, the rainbows, and the sun.

The God of my understanding is everywhere, in everything, and is simply love.

We are all an aspect of God, a thumbprint of the Divine, and so in essence you and God are one and the same. It has been my experience over and over again that we are the Divine, the Creator. Imagine a drop of water in the ocean: Is it a drop of water, or is it the ocean? Each individual drop creates the ocean, just as each individual soul creates the Divine. So, in truth, you have already met God, because you are one and the same. It can take a bit of time to wrap your head around this one. We see this idea phrased another way in this quote:

> When that which is god—or that which is that which man wants to call "God"—is being understood by man, man has to translate it into the format he understands. But this Energy, this Source that man is giving the label of "God," cannot be quantified in anything that man understands. And as man attempts to do it, the distortions are enormous.
>
> —Abraham-Hicks

Visitation during the Death Process

When I was twenty-one years old, my paternal grandfather's health was declining rapidly. He was dying. He had been suffering from congestive heart failure for a few years and had been released from the hospital to live out his last few weeks in the love and comfort of his home. He was happy to be there because he could sleep in his own bed and see his family that he loved dearly. I lived out of state and had a young son, so I wasn't in a position to go and see him, but my grandmother kept us all updated on his condition. I was comforted by the fact that when it got close, my dad would go to be with him.

Three weeks prior to my grandfather's death, I remember my grandmother telling us that Grandpa said someone came to him in a horse and buggy and was ready to pick him up, but he told them he wasn't going. It wasn't his time yet. When my mom and I heard that, we knew his transition was getting closer. When people are in the final stages of life, they often begin to communicate with the spirit world. Family members and friends think they are hallucinating or have perhaps had too much morphine. That is not the case. Most of the time they are beginning to tune in more to the spirit world than the physical world as they begin to disconnect from their physical body. It usually happens more frequently the closer they get to death. So, now that my grandfather was starting to communicate with the spirit world, we knew his spiritual guides were around and preparing to come and get him. It didn't feel immediate, but my mom and I knew it was getting closer, so it was time for my dad to pack his bags and head to Utah to say good-bye to his dad.

Grandpa Anderson, as we all called him, was a very religious man. He was a member of the Mormon Church all of his adult life and served as a visiting teacher. He was an extremely talented graphic artist and made many of the billboards that were along the highways in Utah in the seventies and eighties. He was also the person who came up with the name for the fast-food chain Kentucky Fried Chicken (a fun fact many people don't know). One thing he always had with him or around the house was Werther's Original hard candies. I remember the sweet aroma of caramel wafting through the air whenever I was near him.

I knew many of his external accomplishments, but as I look back, I realize I did not know Grandpa very well. My dad on the other hand, was extremely close to him. When my grandfather was nearing the end, my dad stepped right in and helped with his daily care. His assistance took the pressure off of Grandma, and it was a special time for my dad and Grandpa. My dad slept with him in case he needed anything during the night, and this closeness allowed them both to have as many extra moments with each other as possible.

As the time drew near, my dad awoke during the night and saw Grandpa reaching up with both arms into seemingly thin air. When my dad asked him what he was reaching for, he said, "My mother, she is right here." My dad felt peace knowing that his grandmother was there to help him transition. Grandpa died the next day. His mother had indeed come to take him home.

Within days of his passing, I began to smell that same familiar sent of Werther's Original hard candies that Grandpa loved so much. The scent would show up at random and often meaningful moments. Although I hadn't known my grandfather very well, I discovered after his death that he was keeping a watchful eye on me. At first, I thought this was a bit unusual. Why would he choose to hang out with me, of all people? We were so very different and not particularly close. But then I realized he was teaching me from the other side. Since I was *open* to seeing and feeling and even smelling him, he was showing me that you don't have to be particularly close emotionally to be connected spiritually with someone who passes. This was a very valuable experience for me that I would later teach my students.

People play the exact role that you need in your life, as you do in theirs. Whether you loved someone, hated them, or somewhere in between, when they leave this physical world, they can and often do stay connected. It is interesting to note that the connection is even stronger if you are a namesake.

This was true for me with my grandfather. My middle name, Dawn, is the same as my grandfather's first name, Don. He now serves as a guide for me from the spirit world.

All of these spiritual helpers—from deceased loved ones through to the Divine—are here to help us in life and beyond. We can call on them for assistance throughout our lives on this plane, and they will be there to greet loved ones as they transition. Those who have already crossed over will be there for us, waiting. This group of helpers can include family members, friends, colleagues, even beloved pets. In addition, we will recognize our guardian angel and our spirit guides if we haven't already.

If you've ever been with a family member when they are very near their time of crossing over, you might have noticed they spend a lot of time looking upward. They are seeing light beings. It could be angels, deceased loved ones, spirit guides, or a guardian angel. Everyone has a different experience, so there isn't a one-size-fits-all answer to what they are seeing. But I would say each of them is connecting to the spirit world, recognizing it in some form. Sometimes they also speak about these beings, or reach out to touch them, as my grandfather did with his mother the night before he passed. These spiritual helpers offer a tremendous amount of support and love during this time, as well as offer us continued support as we try to keep communication lines open with those we've loved and lost.

Now that you understand the vibrational levels of the spirit world, it is time to take you on a journey. A journey of hope, freedom, healing, death, peace, closure, pain, and ultimately love. In the next few chapters, I am going to share with you experiences that can only be discovered through the heart connection. You might find the love hiding behind forgiveness, wrapped up in pain, or being denied because of fear. But stay with me, because in each and every story, if you look closely enough, you will find the undeniable message of love in every chapter.

3
Owning Your Gifts

●●●●●●●●●●●●●●●●●●●●●●●●●

Life is eternal; and love is immortal; and death is only a
horizon; and a horizon is nothing save the limit of our sight.
—R. W. Raymond

This book offers many tips on how you can communicate with
your deceased loved ones, but I believe the most important fac-
tor of all is to be present. When you are really present, you can
see, feel, hear, and know the messages that are happening all
around you. I believe that we are all, each and every one of us,
psychic to some degree. It's whether we choose to recognize
and utilize this gift that makes a difference. Anyone who's had
a heart connection with a loved one who has passed has the
natural ability to connect with him or her again. No one has
a closer connection with your deceased loved ones than you
do. By learning to open up to your own intuition, you can continue that relationship with your loved ones who have passed,
and you too will experience the truth that love never ends.

When your loved one dies, it is as if he has moved to China
(the spirit world) and can only speak Mandarin from that point
on. In order to communicate with him, you'll need to learn his
language. The problem is, you don't have any books on Mandarin, so you have to rely on him to teach it to you. This can be

frustrating while you're learning, but you know your loved one is living happily and freely and is just fine. You just miss being able to talk with him or touch him or hear his voice. You may still never see him again, but you can still communicate with him, which brings you so much peace and happiness that you continue living your life with joy because you know that he is as well.

Generally, losing someone we love spurs our interest in the afterlife and mediumship. Experiencing such a significant loss creates a void that we fear will be there forever, never to be filled again. However, if we look beyond the physical to the spiritual and learn to listen with our heart, see through eyes of love, and hear through ears of love, we will realize that our loved ones are right here with us. They have never left us; we just need to learn their new language. I call it the language of love. If you're ready to free yourself from the pain and sadness of not seeing your loved ones who've passed, the first step is understanding your intuition, otherwise known as the clairs.

Note: If you're not ready to attempt communicating with a deceased loved one just yet, if you are still grappling with fear or grief, going through a medium is an excellent choice. A medium is a psychic who has fine-tuned his or her spiritual gifts to such a level that they have the ability to see, hear, feel, and experience spirits from other dimensions who operate at a higher vibration. They are often referred to as a go-between or bridge between the physical world and the spirit world, with the intention being to offer healing to both worlds.

The Clairs

When you are learning to tap into your intuition and the spirit world around you, it is important to understand how the messages will show up. Spirit will send you a message, and your mind and body will begin to experience mental impressions: visions, sounds, feelings, thoughts, and even smells. These are collectively referred to as "the clairs": clairvoyance, clairaudience, clairsentience, claircognizance, and clairfragrance, respectively. You're probably going to notice that your psychic information is delivered in one or two ways most often. To help you determine what your dominant clairs are, let's begin by explaining what they are and how they might show up in psychics or mediums, and of course your own life.

Clairvoyance

Clairvoyance means "clear seeing." This is the ability to see in your mind's eye, called the third eye; a psychic picture or vision of a spirit, object, symbol, or whatever the medium is connecting with during a reading. Clairvoyance is one of the least common, but most desired, of the clairs.

Here are a few ways you might experience clairvoyance:

- Seeing shadows and movements out of the corner of your eye or in your peripheral vision
- Seeing flickering lights of different colors
- Having visions which may come to you as a movie or picture inside or outside of your mind
- Having visions of deceased loved ones or angels
- Seeing images and mental pictures which may come to you in a dream
- Experiencing déjà vu
- Seeing colors and auras
- Having visual signs from heaven, which can be literal or symbolic

Clairaudience

Clairaudience means "clear hearing." This is the use of one's psychic ear—sounds that are heard but are not always physically detectable. In a reading, the psychic or medium might psychically detect or hear voices, music, or other sounds that no one else can.

Here are a few ways you might experience clairaudience:

- Sounds, voices, and words
- The still, small voice within
- A physical or nonphysical voice that you hear inside your heart or head (it might call your name)
- A song on the radio that gives you a message, or a loud voice that comes from nowhere and warns you of danger
- Ringing, buzzing, or popping in your ears
- Music and singing from unidentified sources
- House-settling noises
- Whispers behind you when there is no one there

Clairsentience

Clairsentience means "clear feeling." The feeling can be physical or energetic. A medium can sense when spirits are present and observe their feelings physically and emotionally.

Here are a few ways you might experience clairsentience:

- Chills and goose bumps
- Changes in room temperature; light-headedness
- Feeling a brush against your face
- Tightened stomach muscles

20 North
    Cascade av

1) c,e   3c's
2) c,e   2e
3) c   ?   1d
4) d,e

mostly - feeling
    clairsentient

knowing
clair cogizant

seeing a bit
    clairvoyant

- A feeling of peace or calm
- A gut feeling that you need to do something
- Sudden change in air pressure
- Picking up another's feelings (physical or emotional)

Claircognizance

Claircognizance means "clear knowing." This is when a psychic or medium receives a download of information about a situation or an insight from Spirit instantaneously—usually out of the blue. It is like a telepathic transfer of information. We don't see, hear, feel, or smell this information . . . we just know. This form of clair is probably the most difficult to trust because we wonder how we can "know" something without knowing *how* we know it.

You might experience claircognizance through a sudden:

- Idea
- Concept
- Insight
- Aptitude
- Thought
- Fact

Clairfragrance

Clairfragrance means "clear scent." This is the ability to pick up smells from the psychic nose that are otherwise undetectable by the physical nose. It's common for there to be a fragrance associated with those who are no longer alive and for which no source can be identified.

Sometimes spirits will offer a scent, such as:

- Tobacco smoke
- Perfume
- Flowers
- Baked bread
- Other relevant smells that might be used as a message for validation

The Five Clairs in Action

Your dominant sense is your greatest intuitive gift. Mine is clairsentience; I am a feeler. We are all connected to Spirit; therefore, we all have the ability to use all of our senses. It is imperative that you recognize how you receive your intuitive guidance and then embrace that most dominant sense. In doing so, you own your power as a spiritual being in a human body, and you open the gateway to connect with the spirit world. Everyone can connect to spirit!

The following story illustrates how all five clairs can work together in a single experience to give the most information possible from the spirit world. It is not common to have all five show up in one experience if you are just learning to develop your intuitive gifts. However, once you start building your intuition, just like building a muscle, it will get stronger. As you read through this story, see if you can relate any of your experiences to mine.

Four years ago, my older son Crew was in a car accident. His friend was driving, and they were hit by a woman who had run a red light at forty-five miles per hour. They both sustained some minor cuts and bruising, and they'd also both broken their necks. I had just walked in the door when I saw my husband answer his cell phone. I knew, without him saying a word, that something was wrong with Crew. I jumped back in the car. "Where is he?" I asked.

Thankfully, he was less than a mile away from the house, and we met the firemen and ambulance in the middle of the intersection at the scene of the accident. My son was walking around, saying, "I'm OK, I'm OK," but we knew he wasn't. I forced my way into the ambulance—they weren't taking my baby alone!

We made our way to the hospital, and after several hours of tests, they discovered that he had indeed broken his neck. We stayed overnight, and he was released the next day. Crew chose not to have surgery and is fully functional, with the exception of intermittent neck spasms and pain. But this story isn't about Crew's car accident. It's about what happened afterward.

After a car accident and a hospital stay, dealing with the insurance company naturally follows. I had never filed an insurance claim before, so I had no idea what the process was. I made some initial phone calls while hearing many people tell me how difficult it is to get insurance companies to pay the bills, reimburse you for expenses, etc. I began to feel frustrated, and I'd barely even begun! So, immediately I asked my angels, guides, and helpers to assist me. My exact words were, "Please allow me to walk through this experience with grace and ease, for the highest good of all, and so it is!" Within moments of saying that, I received a call from the claims adjuster and scheduled a follow-up phone call to further discuss the details of the accident. A good sign, I thought.

The day that we were to talk on the phone, I again called in my angels, guides, and helpers to reaffirm my desire. "Please allow me to walk through this experience with grace and ease, for the highest good of all, and so it is!" I repeated this phrase

several times in my mind as I put my headset on and waited for
our appointed time. The claims adjuster began our conversation
by asking for the details of the accident, Crew's injuries, time off
from work, prognosis, etc. As we were talking, I felt a really good
vibe with her, and I sent a little thank-you to Spirit acknowledging the ease I was feeling during our conversation. I didn't know
what everyone was talking about when they said this process was
going to be so hard. So far, this gal was great—or so it seemed.

As soon as I sent my thank-you to Spirit, I felt (clairsentience) the presence of a man in his sixties in my kitchen. I
couldn't see him, but I felt him. I chose to ignore the feeling, as I wanted to focus on the conversation with my claims
adjuster. In order to distract myself, I decided to pour a glass
of iced tea. When I opened my refrigerator, the scent (clairfragrance) of Marlboro Reds drifted out. Shoot, I thought, he's
really trying to communicate with me.

I continued to try to ignore his presence as I poured myself
my iced tea. All of this is happening while the insurance agent
and I, I'll call her Lisa, are still talking. So as you can imagine, I
am distracted with my new "friend," whom I am trying hard to
ignore so I can focus my attention on my phone call. I didn't
want to answer a question incorrectly or miss anything because,
remember, I had heard lots of horror stories about insurance
claims. I was really trying to be present.

I returned the iced tea pitcher to the fridge, and the scent
of Marlboro Reds lingered. Suddenly I know (claircognizance) that this man is Lisa's dad. At this point, I sent up a
not-so-loving message to my angels, guides, and helpers and
reminded them, sternly, that I had asked for grace and ease.
I said, "Don't do this to me right now." I was irritated and not
trusting the bigger picture. I was thinking that Lisa was going
to think I was nuts and wouldn't approve my claim.

I didn't have too much time to sit in my irritation, though, because as I closed the refrigerator door, there he was. Lisa's dad was standing right in front of me. Now I could see (clairvoyance) him, clear as day. At this point I gave in. I realized he was not going anywhere, and I thought to myself that I might as well address him sooner rather than later. So, I got back into my spirit and realized that this moment wasn't about me or my son's claim. I needed to share a message with Lisa that she really needed to hear. I knew what his message was as soon as I tuned into him because he told me (clairaudience).

So, how does one go about sharing a message from the spirit world with someone who knows nothing about this kind of work, isn't asking, and is conducting a professional business call? Well, I'm not sure how you would do it, but I jumped right in.

"Lisa, do you know what I do for a living?"

"No."

"Well, I am a psychic medium. Do you know what that is?"

"*Yes!* I watch that show *Medium* every week. I just love it!!!"

When I heard this, I breathed a sigh of relief and smiled within, knowing that at least I could share the message with her and she had some type of knowledge of the spirit world. Believe it or not, not everyone wants to hear unsolicited messages about their deceased loved ones. It's a fine line, and one I choose not to cross unless Spirit clearly guides me there and I ask permission. I was certainly being led at this time.

I said to Lisa, "I have a message for you from your father if you would like to receive it."

Without skipping a beat she said, "Yes, absolutely, please and thank you. I've been feeling the need to schedule a reading with a medium someday."

I smiled again as I recognized that Spirit had set this up perfectly. Then I apologized to my helpers telepathically for my mistrust and irritation. I was, however, a bit hesitant to share the message, as I knew it was a bit harsh. I just hoped she would be able to hear it.

You see, in my knowing (claircognizance), I learned that her dad had died from lung cancer. I also knew that she was a smoker and was beginning to develop some physical issues herself. Her dad's message was loving but forthright. I asked her one more time, in a different way, if she wanted to hear his message, and she confirmed she did.

I said, "Your father wants you to know how much he loves you. He knows how much you love and miss him. His reason for coming through today, though, is to tell you that you need to quit smoking. He says that if you don't quit, you are going to end up just like him."

I paused and waited for Lisa's response. I could feel the gravity of this message, which was equal to the silence on the other end of the line. After what seemed like ten minutes, but was probably more like two, I could hear sniffles and the sound of a tissue being pulled from the box. Lisa finally responded. "I know. I have been feeling that too."

The acknowledgment of her dad's message did not fall on deaf ears. She heard it with every fiber of her being, and she resonated with it. It was a truth she had looked at previously but denied. Now, with her dad's help, she could choose a different direction. She thanked me profusely. Within minutes, we were back to work, talking about the accident again. At the end of the phone call, she thanked me one more time and said, "I'll be in touch shortly."

I met with Lisa about a week later to sign the paperwork. Everything was taken care of. There was no conflict, no drama, no issues at all. Our claim was settled in an abnormally short amount of time, for the highest good of all, with grace and ease. I thanked my helpers . . . again.

The Clairs Quiz[1]

Still wondering what your dominant sense is? Take this brief test to help you determine it. You can choose one or two answers for each section.

1. If you are in a questioning situation, which of the following might you say?

   a. Something smells fishy to me.

   b. It doesn't sound right to me.

   c. It doesn't feel right to me.

   d. It doesn't look right to me.

   e. I don't think that's right.

2. If you are questioning what another person is saying to you, which of the following might you say?

   a. That idea stinks.

   b. I'm just not hearing what you're trying to say.

   c. I feel differently than you do.

   d. I don't see your point.

   e. I don't think you know what you are saying or talking about.

3. When you're angry, how might you express that?

   a. That person's attitude reeks!

   b. There was a roaring in my ears!

---

1   Adapted with permission from Rhonda Harris-Choudhry and Nathan Bar-Fields's "The Clairs Quiz."

c. I felt so hot/cold/numb

d. I saw red!

e. I thought my head was going to explode!

4. When you're happy, how might you express that?

   a. The smell of happiness is in the air!

   b. Laughter is music to my ears

   c. I feel so great today!

   d. I see a beautiful day ahead of me!

   e. I know today is going to be a fantastic day!

Answers

Now add up the number of a's, b's, c's, d's, and e's that you chose.

Mostly a's: Your dominant sense is smell. You are clairfragrant.

Mostly b's: Your dominant sense is hearing. You are clairaudient.

Mostly c's: Your dominant sense is feeling. You are clairsentient.

Mostly d's: Your dominant sense is seeing. You are clairvoyant.

Mostly e's: Your dominant sense is knowing. You are claircognizant.

You can have more than one dominant sense. It is typical to have a dominant sense and then a secondary one. For example, if you chose three a's and one d, then your dominant sense is smell and your secondary sense is sight.

This quiz helps you to discern your most dominant attribute or gift. Remember, however, that it is very likely that you have had, at one time or another, experiences in all of these areas. We are just looking for the strongest gift, the most natural one.

Why does it matter what your strongest natural intuitive gift is? Well, in order to really fine-tune your intuition, to raise your vibration up enough to connect with your loved ones that have passed, you need to be aware of how they will be trying to contact you. If you know your dominant attribute, you will better recognize the signs when they begin to communicate with you. You will be aware and you will have no doubt about their presence and that your love lives on. The main goal your deceased loved ones have in wanting to connect with you is to help you move on, free of the pain, regret, and grief, so that you can live your life in joy and peace, and complete your own life lessons.

Quiet the Mind

The spirit world connects with us through thoughts and feelings, so those who have passed can tune into our emotions. They often come around when we think of them. In fact, you can line your energy up to allow yourself to see or feel them. However, when your loved ones come into your mind or heart seemingly out of the blue, Spirit tells me that's them sending you a hello.

One big step in initiating this connection is by meditating or practicing automatic writing. The following simple exercises will help you get tuned in, present, and quiet. These can be used daily, weekly, or anytime you feel like something is shifting within you and you need more clarity, guidance, or connection with the spirit world.

Meditation

Meditation is a technique that is often used to receive guidance, focus energy, and gain clarity. There are various forms of meditation, so choose what works best for you. Some people focus on the breath, others on an affirmation, others on a vision. The end goal for all, though, is to attain stillness. For when we are still, we are present; and when we are present, we can hear the spirit world much more clearly.

I would encourage you, if you desire to connect with your loved ones on the other side, to make meditation part of your spiritual practice. Whether it is for five minutes or fifty minutes is not important. It is only important to do it consistently. As with anything, the more consistently you practice, the stronger you will become at it, and the stronger your connection to the spirit world will become as well.

Don't wait until you have the time—it'll never happen. Let's begin now.

Create a space where you will not be interrupted for at least a half hour. No cell phone or computer. Nothing to distract you from the stillness. Make sure this is a safe and comfortable environment for you. You may want to have some sacred objects beside you, such as crystals, deities, incense, or a lit candle. If you desire to connect with a loved one who has passed over, maybe one or two of their items or a picture of them would be good, too. It is your space, so create it to fit your energy and personality. I would suggest having a journal and a pen beside you for notes afterward as well. A computer is fine, but have it off during the meditation.

Sit in a comfortable position. There are many suggested ways to sit. Many of them are also uncomfortable. Sit in whatever way is comfortable for you. On the floor or on a chair, even laying down is fine.

If you feel so guided, take a moment to ask the God of your understanding, your angels, spirit guides, or deceased loved ones for assistance in connecting with Spirit. If this is new to you, you can ask Archangel Gabriel, who helps with communication, and/or Archangel Uriel, who helps with seeing the greater vision, for support and guidance.

Clear your mind. Release the tension from your body. Relax by focusing on your breath. Take a nice, deep breath in, and hold it for seven seconds. Then breathe out for seven seconds. Let your breath become your focus. Repeat this for a few minutes, until you feel your mind's chatter begin to die down.

Now just observe. Be a witness to your thoughts and feelings. Allow them to just drift in and out, like clouds. As the love comes in, you are becoming aware of what has always been there, but has been hidden by the thousands of other thoughts and feelings you are experiencing on a daily basis. The more aware you are, the quieter your mind becomes so that you can really be in touch with the quiet connection within.

As you breathe in and out, keep letting those everyday thoughts drift away. Allow yourself to go deeper within, reaching that stillness where Spirit speaks to you and reveals the messages you need to hear.

When you feel complete, recharged, or disconnected, take a few deep breaths and slowly return back to your space. Open your eyes.

Now take a moment and write down anything that stays with you, anything you feel deep within. This is the guidance of your spirit. You can do this every day, keeping notes on what the messages are as you continue your meditation practice.

Please remember, the more you meditate, the deeper you will go, and the easier it will get. Practice, practice, practice, and as that stillness comes to you, it moves through you. With commitment and consistency, your connection with Spirit will begin to reveal itself more and more.

Automatic Writing

Automatic writing is the practice of channeling your subconscious or the spiritual world and recording those words without intention or input. It dates back to Victorian times, and you can practice it anytime you are in need of insight and connection.

As I have discovered, your purpose is constantly changing as you change and grow and expand. So, this exercise may be helpful at any given time along your journey of life. Automatic writing will help you to be conscious of what is calling to you at this particular time in your life so that you can live intentionally and consciously. Let's begin.

Create a space where you will not be interrupted for at least an hour (no cell phone or computer for this activity either).

Have a couple of sheets of paper and a pen ready. No computer keyboard for this one, please.

If you feel so guided, take a moment to ask the God of your understanding, your angels, spirit guides, or any other deities for assistance in connecting with Spirit. You may want to specifically call on Archangel Gabriel to help you with greater communication.

At the top of your paper, write a question. It can be any question you would like more information on. Here are a few examples:

- What message does the spirit world have for me?
- What do I need to know about _____ today?
- What sign does Grandpa use to show me that he is with me?

- Why do I get goose bumps at seemingly random times?

Now write anything and everything that comes into your awareness. Write without editing and without stopping. I call this stream-of-consciousness writing. It can be words, sentences, phrases—even pictures. As you write, observe your emotions and the feelings you have in your body. Don't judge or interpret any of the messages—this is very important—just write it all down.

Continue writing until you feel complete or clear, it has been over a half hour, or you have a lot of emotion.

Once you've finished, go through your writing and note what brings up the most emotion in you. The messages that you can really feel in your heart. The ones that resonate with you. The ones that make you cry. The ones that give you the chills. These messages, words, and sentences are validation of truth for you. It is Spirit speaking to you.

Sometimes people question if automatic writing is really angelic guidance or a deceased loved one reaching out. My experience is that if it is a higher vibrational message that brings you comfort, support, or love, it is a message from the spirit world. It then becomes a process of discerning whom it is from: your guardian angel, a spirit guide, or a loved one. If you listen closely, you will intuitively know whom it is from. Trust your intuition, it is your greatest guide to communication with the spirit world.

Dreams

It is very common in the first few months for people to have dreams of their departed loved ones. When we sleep, our vibration rises, and the dream state is the time when we have the least amount of (or maybe no) resistance. Therefore, it is the easiest time for spirits to connect with us, because they don't have to lower their vibration for us to feel them. Communicating through dreams is a simpler way to begin a conversation, so it's usually how they start the dialogue—especially when someone has recently transitioned. Most people don't realize this is spirit communication, however; they think they are just having a dream about their deceased loved one. The truth is, it is not a dream. They are actually connecting with their deceased loved ones, in that vibrational space.

There have been so many times when a client has had a dream of his or her deceased loved one and then made an appointment with me to help them understand either what the dream meant or to validate that it really was their loved one. It is an extremely common occurrence, and I would say that, 95 percent of the time, their loved ones on the other side not only validate that it was them, but give answers to prove that this can be a new way of communication between the two of them.

One client, Agnes, had been dreaming about her husband every night since he had passed away. She loved having the dreams because she felt "almost as if he wasn't really gone." But when she would awaken, she would realize that it was just a dream, and her sadness and heartbreak would begin again. In this case, her husband *was* coming to her in her dreams, to help her to see that he really wasn't gone. Her heart was correct when she felt her husband was still with her; but in her own head, she was feeling it was just plain mean to take him away and then bring him back and take him away again every morning. She felt as though Spirit was just teasing her, when really her husband's spirit was trying instead to reassure her. He was trying to remind her of a truth that she knew deep within but wasn't able to believe in. He wasn't really gone, and her dream state was actually her first contact in restoring that heart connection.

Another woman, Paulette, had been dreaming about her son Sam since his death at the age of six. In her dreams, he was always telling her how much he loved her in a variety of different ways. In one, he made her a sign that said, "I love you, Mommy." In another, he sang her a little love ditty. In yet another, he would hug her as tight as he could and just wouldn't let go. Every dream would have a different message of love. Paulette was happy to have the dreams, but more than anything she wanted to never wake up. Yet, morning would come, and the peace and joy that filled her dream state would then be replaced with the reality of her life: Her son was dead. She would wake up and spend the next sixteen hours waiting for the next dream. It became a dangerous cycle.

During our reading, I shared with Paulette that in these dreams, her son was trying to share the messages that he couldn't give to her in person during his last several months of life, because he was incapable of communication. With that realization, her heart immediately brightened. And when she discovered, through her son communicating with me, all the other ways he had been visiting her, she began to beam. I watched as light was literally just pouring in and radiating out of her. You see, Paulette had been so depressed; she was not present in life, in any way. So she had missed the signs he was sending her all along. Once she realized that he truly was with her, not just in the dream state but in the focused presence of everyday life, she became lighter right before my eyes. She had a reason to live again. A few minutes later, as our session concluded, Paulette almost floated out of my office—and into a newfound relationship with her beloved son.

Early Signs That Your Loved Ones Are Trying to Connect

As your departed loved ones begin to heal and grow and expand, and as they learn more in their new world, they evolve from showing up in the dream state to other means of communication. They also begin to experiment with expressing themselves in different ways. They may start showing signs like a butterfly, a rose, or a heart; they might call your phone but no one will be there (or, better yet, a call will come from their old number); they might push pictures off the shelves; they might send you impressions in your heart, mind, and body.

Sometimes, it can be hard to determine whom the message is from—especially if it's open to interpretation. Perhaps you've had two very close family members (say, your brother and your father) pass away. You can feel someone around, but how do you figure out who is trying to communicate with you? This can be challenging. It takes discernment, which is not something that can be taught. It must be experienced. So, it takes practice.

First, see if you get a clear sense of who it is. Sometimes it is that easy. Second, when you feel the presence of Spirit, tune into who comes into your heart and mind first, and that is likely who's trying to reach you. Your intuition is usually right on. Third, ask for confirmation. Ask Spirit to show you a sign that it is the person you are thinking of . . . and then pay attention. This confirmation can be something like having their picture fall off the wall, or having someone with the same name call you, or seeing a license plate that reminds you of them. If you ask for a sign and pay attention to your intuition, Spirit will provide you with validation.

You may find that once you're tuned in, you receive consistent messages from one person but not the other. Each spirit has its own purpose in connecting with you; therefore, just like humans, some may not feel it necessary to connect. There are a variety of reasons why this might happen:

- They may see that you are doing fine and want you to continue carrying on with your life.
- They may be focusing their attention on other people.
- They may be learning the ropes in their new home.
- They may be sending you messages, and you just aren't picking them up yet because they are different than the way the other spirits are sending them.
- You are simply unaware of the messages from the spirit world.

My advice would be to stay open to receiving the messages in whatever form they may appear. This is not something that you can control. Believe me, I've tried.

Oftentimes, before someone passes away they make agreements to continue communicating after they are gone. The conversation usually goes something like, "Grandma, when you get to the spirit world show me a butterfly, and I will know it is you." This creates an intention to keep the lines of communication open. It's certainly OK to make those kinds of suggestions, but it isn't necessary. All you need to do is stay present for all the ways they might be communicating with you—and not only the one or two ways you talked about beforehand. Once your loved one goes home, he or she has to learn to focus their attention enough to get us those messages, and sometimes in the beginning there are ways that might be easier for them to communicate with us. I have had many clients who are looking for one sign and later realize they missed ten others . . . so just be sure to stay open for any and all signs.

Above all else, the one thing we can do to hear our loved ones more clearly is to raise our vibration. That is the fastest way to communicate with them. Sometimes it is helpful to be able to do some psychometry (obtaining information psychically about a person or event by touching a related object) with an item of theirs. That can help connect you with their energy. But most importantly, get into a place of feeling your love for them . . . and you will sense them.

4
Helping Someone Transition without Fear

I'm not afraid of death because I don't believe in it. It's just getting out of one car, and into another.

John Lennon

Janie was a unique gal, a real tough chick. Dedicated and strong-willed, she taught shooting classes for the NRA and was employed as a full-time police officer, where she investigated crime scenes at fatal car accidents in Arizona. In all areas of her life she was a woman prepared to go above and beyond for her job and her family. Given her stressful occupation, it was no surprise that she enrolled in my meditation class.

We always ended each meditation class in a circle, holding hands as we sent each other energy. I would walk around the outside of the circle and lay my hands on each student, sending them love, blessings, and Reiki. Over a few sessions, I began to notice that Janie's energy seemed to be becoming more and more depleted. Her vibration felt lower, and I sensed some physical illness or disease in her body. When I asked her about it, she just passed it off as working too much.

After a couple more weeks of this, I confronted her. "Janie, what's going on? You aren't yourself." All she would tell me was that she was having some health problems. She was too proud to ask for help or even let anyone know there was an issue. She made me promise her that I wouldn't say anything to anyone, and I didn't. Each week, I continued to send her love and light, always feeling guided to focus the energy on her head. I could sense something was going on there, but I wasn't sure exactly what it was. I knew it was serious when she quit coming to class and she wouldn't return my calls.

It was four months later that I received a phone call from her daughter, Geri. She said, "Sunny, I don't know if you know, but my mother has brain cancer and now it has spread into her lungs. I am hoping you will come with some of your students or colleagues and do whatever it is that you do."

I knew that if Janie had given her daughter my number, she must be very sick. Over the next couple days I gathered some people who knew and loved Janie and we went to her house. We weren't prepared for how sick Janie was. She was upbeat and happy to see us, but her energy was *soooo* low. She had put a little makeup on, and had a babushka covering her little bald head. She tried to hide her fear and even her sickness, but it was evident by her frail body that she was very ill.

We spent the afternoon doing Reiki and helping her get comfortable. We tried to talk to Janie about her illness, but she wasn't willing to acknowledge it. When the subject of death came up, she said quite sternly, "*I am not dying.* I still have a lot to do." I acknowledged her truth and we left it right there. That was the second week of December. Her daughter called later that afternoon and said that she hadn't seen Janie that upbeat in a long time and asked me to come back the day after Christmas.

A few days before Christmas, I woke up thinking about Janie. I had a bad feeling. I called Geri just to check in, and she said that Janie was going downhill fast. The doctors didn't think she had much time left, and she asked if I could come the following day.

The next morning, I asked Spirit to guide me. I was a bit nervous knowing that Janie was near death, and I wanted to be a source of comfort to her and her family. As I got out of the car, Spirit guided me to take Deva Premal's CD *The Essence* with me. As soon as I got there, I climbed right in bed with her and lay next to her. She was in a coma now and wasn't able to communicate verbally, but she said a lot telepathically.

I began talking to Janie about the people she would see who would be there to help her cross over—family members and friends who loved her. As I telepathically expressed that to her, I heard her say, "Nope, I am not going anywhere." It was hard to see her so weak but hanging on so tight. Janie was *not* going anywhere—not yet, anyway. She still had things to do.

After a few hours, I went into the dimly lit kitchen and spoke with Janie's husband and daughter. I told them there was something that was not complete and that she told me she wasn't going because she still had things to do. The husband looked at me a little funny, but I pushed on. I asked if everyone had been by to see her, and they said yes, over the past week or two everyone had come by.

I went back into the bedroom to meditate and connect with Spirit to see if I could get an answer to why she was hanging on. It was so painful to watch, and it seemed so unnecessary. Even though I believe that everything happens for a reason, I was questioning what this reason could possibly be. "Why?" I asked Spirit. "Why?"

As I sat in meditation, Spirit guided me to pick some angel cards for guidance. But the sound of the death rattle from Janie took me out of my meditation, and I turned my attention back to her. I asked her again what she was waiting for. I reassured her that it was OK to go and that she would not feel any pain. I knew she wasn't scared, but I couldn't figure out why she was staying. I was desperate to do something to help her. It was then that I was reminded to pick the angel cards.

I said a prayer and pulled three cards. The cards were "Surrender and Release," "New Love," and "Celebration." From there, the message I received was that Janie was holding on for someone. And being as strong-minded as she was, she wasn't leaving until she had closure.

Who could it be? I wondered. I went out and talked to Geri again. I told her that I believed there was someone who was having a hard time letting her go. She acknowledged, through tears running down her face, that they all were. But it wasn't one of them. They were all here. This was someone else. That's when Geri said, "I bet it's my uncle, Janie's brother." They had asked him to come back and see her one last time, but he wouldn't. He just couldn't stand to see her like that.

I asked Geri to call her uncle one more time and tell him that Janie was waiting for him. As long as it took, she would wait. Janie was that stubborn. I told her to appeal to his love for her, not his fear. He needed to come and see her, and then she could let go. This message from Janie and Spirit had been very clear, and I was insistent. Geri didn't think he would come, but she agreed to call him one more time.

I went back in with Janie, feeling more clear about why she was hanging on. As I walked in, I felt a lot of spirits in the room. Her mother and father were there. I felt that this support coming in meant she was ready to go; but her spirit told me she wasn't going anywhere unless her brother came.

I put the Deva Premal CD on and listened to my favorite song, "Gayatri Mantra." As I lay there next to her, "Om Asatoma" came on. This was a song that I had never really heard before. It was like Spirit was whispering an important message to me, which gave me chills from head to toe. Although the song is sung in Sanskrit (the language of the spirit world) and I didn't understand a word of it, I could feel its significance. So, I picked up the jacket of the CD and read that this song was a mantra to be sung in transitional periods of life, and especially in preparation for the ultimate transition, death. The English translation was the following:

> Lead me to the understanding that I am not the limited body, mind and intellect, but am, was and always will be that eternal, absolute, blissful consciousness that serves as their substratum.

The truth of that passage resonated with me so deeply that all I could do was cry. My tears were out of love, not sadness.

I hit repeat on the CD player and suggested to Geri that they keep it playing. With that validation, it was time for me to go. I had done what I came to do. I had planted the seeds of suggestion, and now I just needed to get out of the way. I kissed Janie good-bye, knowing that this would be our last meeting—in this physical life, anyway. She was in good hands.

Geri called me later that evening to tell me that Janie's brother came about an hour after I had left. He was afraid to see her, but he was willing, and he quickly popped into the bedroom to say "Hey, Janie, I'm here." He gave her a kiss on the forehead and said "I will be right back." He went into the restroom to compose himself, and when he returned Janie had transitioned. Geri was in shock, amazed by how quickly Janie passed once her brother arrived.

Now that would seem to be the end of the story . . . but there was one question left unanswered: Why was it so important for

Janie to stay until she saw her brother? I was curious and asked Geri if she knew. She shared with me, through her tears, how close Janie and her brother were and how much they both loved their mother. About ten years earlier, Janie's brother had planned a motorcycle trip, and his mother was very ill. He didn't know if he should leave, but because she had been sick for so long, he decided to go. It was just an overnight trip, but when he returned, their mother had died. He had never forgiven himself for not being there with her. The guilt had eaten away at everything he loved. As a matter of fact, he hadn't ridden his motorcycle since that day. Janie was *not* going to allow him to beat himself up like he did when their mom passed. Her love for her brother was stronger than any disease. She was not going to leave until he came to see her, so that she could help him heal from his mother's death by creating a different experience. In her final act, Janie showed her brother the path to forgiveness, and I heard that shortly after Janie's death, her brother started riding his motorcycle again.

There may be times when we will not understand why our loved ones are hanging on, and it can be difficult to witness someone holding on so tight—especially if they are in pain. It could be that they are waiting to give family members or friends the opportunity to resolve issues before they pass. It could also be that they are doing some of their own work before they transition. But we have to find a way to trust that all is in divine time. If we are divine beings, God sparks, Spirit embodied, then we know, on a soul level, when it is time to go. We as humans have to learn to believe this as well.

I learned through Janie that Spirit sees a greater picture and understands much more that we do. We have to learn to trust. Everything is happening for a reason. Someone in a coma is serving a purpose, but you might have to get out of your head and into your heart to see it.

Janie's strength was a blessing to her family and everyone around her. But there will be times when each of us will be called upon to comfort the sick, and it's one of the biggest tasks—and gifts—we'll ever experience. When you find yourself caring for someone who's very sick, or who is dying of old age, share with them what you've learned in this book. Send them love, send them light, pray for them, call in the angels, and see them in the truth of who they are—love.

Love is what heals them and us. Help them to understand that love never ends, and that they will still be with you, just from another point of view. Teach them about the absolutely blissful place they are going to: the beautiful light vibration that words cannot even express, the sounds that are so harmonic you just can't get enough, and the love that is out of this world. Once you have shared, you must let them find their own way and honor that way. Whether they go in fear or they go in love, love is waiting for them on the other side. This truth can bring you both peace.

5
Coping with a Traumatic Death

• •

You were born a child of light's wonderful secret—you
return to the beauty you have always been.
—Aberjhani, *Visions of a Skylark Dressed in Black*

Death can sometimes come without warning. In these cases, it's important to remember that the person about to cross over could be fearful of the transition, and they also have had no time to prepare for it. The following story shares my experience of comforting someone in such a situation.

In August 2001, I was preparing for a workshop on divine guidance. While organizing my thoughts onto paper, I got a call from my friend Mary, who said she was coming up for the workshop. She then asked me if I could meet her at Sam's Club before the workshop. I told her no, I was still in my PJs and getting prepared for class. It wouldn't work for me today. She begged me. She didn't have a Sam's card and really needed to go with someone. She suggested we meet there for lunch and then at least eating would be taken care of. I said I'd think about it and hung up the phone feeling irritated that she wouldn't let it go.

I wasn't sure if it was my guilt or what, but I found myself calling Mary back and telling her I'd meet her at Sam's Club. I didn't have any extra time, but I had this feeling I couldn't shake, and if I was teaching on the topic of divine guidance that night, I thought I should probably listen and follow my own.

I finished getting dressed, and ten minutes later I met Mary at Sam's Club. A few minutes in, we heard an announcement over the loudspeaker asking whether there were any doctors or nurses in the building, and if so, to please come to the front entrance. We were near the entrance but couldn't see anything from where we were. Mary kept shopping while I began to wander toward the door. I'm not a nurse or doctor, but I am curious, and I could feel something serious happening. Spirit was guiding and I was listening; I didn't need to know why.

When I got to the front of the building, I saw a large man in his forties on the ground and several people around him. I was guided to move toward a young man who looked to be in his early twenties standing outside the door with his head in his hands. I could see he was visibly upset. I walked up to him and said, "I am a minister, would you like me to pray for your friend or to pray with you?" He responded with a sense of urgency in his voice and said, "Yes, please do whatever you can do for my friend."

With the young man's permission, I walked over to the older man lying on the floor and sat down next to him and held his hand. I knew as soon as I sat down that he was getting ready to pass. I felt his spirit hovering over his body, and I could feel the presence of other souls gathering to help him cross over. I could also feel his fear. I told him telepathically that if it was his time to go, it was OK. He didn't need to be afraid. I just kept reassuring him that he was safe, loved, and that it was OK to go to the light.

As I sat there with this stranger, I felt as if we were one. We were so connected, and I was honored to be a part of this sacred moment. As I closed my eyes and tuned into his spirit, I felt it leave through my own body.

Our sacred moment ended quickly when the paramedics rushed in and applied an oxygen mask and checked his vital signs. I stayed by his side and held his hand as I continued to ask the angels to be with him. Although I knew he was gone and the medics were working on an empty shell, I felt as though I needed to stay connected to him to honor the sacred space we had just moved through. The paramedics just kept saying, "I have stats on him. I have stats on him." I didn't voice anything, but I was really confused. How could they have readings on him? I knew he was already gone.

I am not knowledgeable about emergency medicine, so I didn't know that they were saying he still had a chance to live. But I knew he was already gone. My thoughts were still racing when the paramedic yelling "Get the shot!" brought me back to the present moment. They pulled this huge needle out of their kit and pushed it straight into his heart.

"He is dead, he's gone," I mumbled to no one but myself. I sat by his side, still holding his hand, knowing that at this point it was more for my comfort than his. Then they put him on a stretcher and rushed him away. I finally had a chance to take a breath.

I gathered myself and walked outside to see Mary waiting there patiently for me. We hugged for a moment, in awe of what had just happened. I then felt a powerful urge to talk to the man's friend, who introduced himself as Kent. I learned the man on his way to the hospital was named Jim. He was a very close friend of the family. Kent actually referred to him as an uncle. Kent had basically watched his dear friend die of a heart attack on the floor of Sam's Club.

"Do you think he is going to be OK?" he asked me. I couldn't answer. My solemn face gave the answer away, though, and Kent began to cry. As he cried I tried to convince myself that I might be wrong about what I had just witnessed and felt. Miracles happen every day, I told myself. But my heart knew the truth. Jim was gone. I gave Kent a hug as he thanked me for all I had done. I asked him to please call me later that evening to let me know what happened.

As I drove home, I felt surprisingly calm and relaxed. I began to realize that my experience that afternoon had given me a profound insight: When it is our time, it is our time. No matter where we are, what we are doing, or whom we are with, when our time is up, it's up. This is kind of scary to think about, but also freeing, in a way.

People sometimes wonder about having a near-death experience. How does that fit with the idea of when your time is up, it's up? My thought is, if we come back, then it was wasn't our time to go and it was just an experience to learn from. It's an opportunity to grow and rethink our priorities and remember the value of life. This experience was an example that everything really does happen for a reason. I was there for a reason.

I sat there in awe of the Universe. All the work I was going to do. All that planning I felt I needed to have. Everything I had intended to talk about. They were just words, not experience. The Universe had given me an opportunity to experience divine guidance firsthand, and I was beyond grateful. That night I dedicated my class to Jim. I shared from experience, not written word, on how divine guidance works. I received a standing ovation.

The next day Kent called to tell me that Jim had passed away that afternoon at the store. He was declared dead upon arrival. He again thanked me for all I had done and asked if I would come to Jim's funeral. He said that Jim had several brothers and sisters who would like to meet me because I was with him when he died. They wanted to be able to thank me in person and hear more about his experience. I felt honored. Kent also assured me that this wasn't going to be a drab, dreary funeral. This was going to be a party.

As I drove into the parking lot, I saw lots of Harley-Davidson motorcycles and a group of people hanging outside, smoking cigarettes and belly laughing. I wasn't sure what to expect as I walked up to the funeral home, but I knew it wouldn't be boring. As I entered, I felt a bit insecure, as I was the only one in a suit. (Isn't that what everyone wears to a funeral? you might ask. Not this one!) I was definitely the odd one of the bunch. Everyone attending wore bandanas, handkerchiefs, and leather. It was such a beautiful expression of love to their friend Jim, as I later learned that he loved motorcycles, sports, and jeans. They were honoring him by wearing what he would wear. It was definitely the most colorful service I had ever been to, and one I will never forget. Recalling their expression of love always puts a smile on my face. However, it was the words of Jim's sister that still live in my heart and make me cry as I write this today.

She thanked me for being there, and as she spoke, tears filled her eyes. She revealed that she and her siblings had talked about it at great length, and they all believed that I was an angel sent there that day to be with Jim so that he didn't have to die alone. They believed that when I got down on that floor and he looked at me, he felt my love. He knew he was in the arms of an angel and he had no fear and could be guided home. Jim lived alone and never married or had children, but he loved people and always wanted to be around people. One of his fears, she shared with me, was dying alone.

When she'd finished talking, Jim's sister hugged me tight and whispered in my ear, "Thank you for being our angel too. We are at peace because we know he was." I felt so blessed. The love I felt for this stranger, I can't explain it. Why I decided to go to Sam's Club, I can. It was divine guidance.

Jim and I had a divine appointment, and I am forever grateful to him for choosing to share his last moments with me. Our spirits were connected to allow both of us to expand that day. I could provide him comfort and encouragement to walk through his fear and ease his transition. He gave me an experience that I continue to share and teach from even now. I know that we can and will be divinely guided by messages from beyond. These messages come not from our head, but from our heart. They will always lead us to our highest good, if we only will allow ourselves to listen.

In deaths that are premature, there is a moment where the spirit recognizes that it is either time to turn back or to continue forward on the journey home. The best way that I can describe what I have felt and seen is that as the spirit is released from this earthly plane, it is almost like it is sucked up, like a vacuum. Remember that the spirit is energy, so there is no form. It's as if that energy shoots up this light vibrational suction cup or tube of sorts. The tube is complete light . . . awe-inspiring, indescribable, vibrating beams of brilliant light that feels to me like absolute love and healing.

At the moment of death, we release all resistance and form. This transition, I've heard, feels like you are being pulled or lifted from your body, straight up. I've also heard it described as feeling very similar to going to sleep. The point of transition isn't painful at all. It is a complete and absolute release of resistance. That doesn't mean that people don't feel pain during the death process, and we all try to help them through this as best we can, but at the actual point of transition, the pain is gone.

If a loved one transitions before you're able to be by his or her side, know that your love is absolutely felt from a distance—as well as your guilt. It is best if you can try to focus on your love, for both of your sakes. If circumstances make it so that you aren't able to be present, then that was part of the divine plan, which they now know. They know you tried to get there; and oftentimes, honestly, they don't want anyone there. They want to be alone. The way it is often revealed to me is that the process will unfold in the way that they want it. So if you are there, or not, it is in perfect divine order.

While it is painful to say good bye, we can help ease some of that pain by being supportive of those who are about to move on, knowing that this is not the end. You can communicate with your departed loved ones immediately after their passing if you are able to raise your vibration and be open. It takes a lining up of energy, and that can take a little time to coordinate, but not too long. If you aren't ready to go it alone, you could enlist the help of a medium to resume communication soon. Or, if you're ready, you can begin looking for the signs almost immediately. The bottom line is, spirit is always spirit. We just receive a body when we are here, and leave it when we go—but we are communicating all the while.

Suicide Teaches about Love

I met Randy and Marcia when I was speaking at the Celebrate Your Life conference in Scottsdale, Arizona, about six years ago. They were a beautiful couple, just married and embarking on a new journey together. Marcia became a dear student of mine, and we saw each other on a pretty regular basis at classes and events. I didn't know Randy as well, but I loved him and his sweet, sensitive nature.

When the couple hosted one of my living room book tours in their home in January 2011, I got to know the entire family on a more personal level. From that point, both Marcia and Randy came to individual retreats, and I had the opportunity to experience and witness their personal and relationship challenges. By August 2012, they had separated, and Randy was desperate. He signed up for my healing retreat as a last-ditch effort to ease his pain and heartbreak.

When he showed up, he seemed like he had all but given up on his relationship, and, even more importantly, himself. Thankfully, throughout the retreat he met some amazing people, built some fabulous relationships, and had some great aha moments and insights into his own struggles and behaviors. He left the retreat with a new zest for life, a reestablished connection with his deceased father, and an unmistakable joy about a future he could create for himself. He said several times that he needed to learn to live for him, and when he left, it seemed that he had joy in his heart and a new awareness of himself. Outwardly, he appeared excited to get on with his life and was in a good place to be able to do that.

Over the next several months, however, I didn't hear from Randy. Intuitively I knew that he wasn't doing well. I had tried to reach out to him a few times with no response. I checked in with Marcia, who confirmed my worst fears. Randy had fallen back into a depressed state and was isolating himself from friends and family. "He's just not himself," Marcia said. In January he was fired from his job, and five days later his family found his body. He had been dead for several days.

I got the call on Monday at 11 a.m., and all I was told was that Randy was missing. No one had heard from him for two days, and he hadn't responded to numerous text messages and phone calls. I got a sick feeling that rippled through my body . . . a familiar feeling. One year ago to the day, my husband's best friend, and a brother, really, had taken his own life. I recall feeling that same feeling I had the year before. I *knew* Randy was dead. I don't know if it was his suicide that was more shocking or that it was the exact same day one year later. Regardless, I couldn't believe it was happening again. I had thought about how my husband and I would spend the first anniversary of our dear friend's death, but once the news came and Randy's body was found, I found myself walking the same journey I had the year before. It really was unbelievable!

I was in a bit of a haze the first few minutes after I found out, and then myriad phone calls began coming in. So many people in disbelief . . . again. Tears of sadness and loss rippled through our hearts. My initial shock turned to sadness, and then very quickly I turned my attention to Marcia. As we talked, I could feel her heart breaking in two, and I knew what I needed to do.

I went over to Marcia's house that night, climbed in bed with her, and just held her for a little while. We talked for a couple of hours and made some plans through a million tears and hundreds of Kleenex.

Plans are difficult to make in these circumstances, and what was remarkable to me was Marcia's consideration for everyone else and her unending, unconditional love for Randy. This woman was walking a journey no one would ever want to walk. It is likely one of the most difficult experiences in this physical life, separating from your partner, whom you love, and then losing them, especially in this way. I observed her love and compassion for everyone involved, even in the middle of the shock of those first twenty-four hours.

Randy had orchestrated his own death, taking great care to make sure every detail was taken care of. When they found his body, he was lying on a plastic covering on top of the bed that he took his last breath in. They also discovered insurance papers on the table. It appeared as though he had painstakingly scoured through his life, arranging everything that would be needed after his death in order to make it easier on those he loved so dearly. Unfortunately, nothing that he planned made it any easier for his wife and loved ones. Just knowing how much pain he must have been in to execute such an elaborate death was devastating to them all. Questions of what they could have done, how they could have stopped it lurked behind their every thought. From Randy's perspective, he was acting out of love for his family. Unfortunately, he had lost that beautiful self-love that I had seen just a few months earlier. Randy would later share through a letter how blind he was to love in his life because of self-hate and rejection, and how sorry he was that he couldn't see it. I realized that we had begun a new journey of understanding and compassion, with Randy at the helm, although his family and friends didn't know it yet!

Tragedies like this show different sides of people. Suicide in particular can rock you to your core. It absolutely changes who you are. The changes can be positive or not, depending on the person and their choices throughout the journey. It is easy to go to a place of guilt and shame, to be angry and vengeful at the perceived faults of others. It is easy to blame and hate. It is easy to give up on God, life, and everything that once mattered. It is easy to want to hide from the truth that suicide brings. It is easy to wish yourself dead as well. These are all reasonable feelings, feelings that some people never move through. It is much harder to stand up, hold your head high, pull that unconditional love in from the depths of your heart and soul, and just love. This is what Marcia did, though. She loved!

Marcia was a strong Latina woman; compassionate, loving, joyful, driven, very intuitive and aware. What I didn't know was how this journey would change her, how the depths of despair would affect her strong spirit and how the painful memories of Randy would pummel her. Where would replaying the last few days and weeks of his life take her? I have been a witness to several clients and friends in similar experiences, and I knew where she could possibly go. However, what I witnessed was an exceptionally strong and courageous woman who became, for many, an example of how to walk this undeniably difficult journey with grace and unconditional love.

Over the next few days Marcia and I spoke on the phone several times a day and met a couple of times in person as well. She realized, through Randy's encouragement and support from the other side, how important it was to ask for help; and in her asking, there were many people who stepped up to help. She was offered counseling, mediumship, a massage, Reiki, food to eat, and friends to talk to. The help showed up in so many ways. This is such an important thing to remember for those who are grieving the loss of someone: Asking for and receiving help is an absolute must.

Marcia was listening to Randy's guidance, and he came through several times with messages of love and an apology for all the pain he had caused her not just in death, but in life. He reinforced how important it was that we take care of ourselves, something he hadn't been so good at, which had eventually led him to resentment and isolation. Marcia now had a choice, and a greater awareness because of Randy's death, and she chose to follow through by taking care of herself. Not an easy feat in this type of situation, but critical for her own healing.

I believe that part of the reason Marcia could walk through this journey with such love, grace, and dignity was because of the spiritual connection she and Randy had. Yes, they certainly had challenges as a couple, but there was something greater that connected them. It was a very deep and special bond they shared, perhaps that of a soul mate.

When it was time to prepare for the funeral, Marcia asked me to officiate. I invited Marcia and her family to come to my office so we could plan the service and the celebration. When they arrived, I was in awe, as there were several carloads of people. I saw Marcia's two children, whom I had met several times, and a whole bunch of others, and they were all speaking Spanish. As they walked into my office, Marcia introduced me to Randy's three sons, two family friends, his brother, his mother, and his ex-wife, who was the mother of his sons.

I was amazed by the love that I witnessed Marcia sharing with Randy's family. And the love Marcia had for Randy became even more evident as we talked about his life, his death, and everything in between. Randy came through during the meeting, making it clear that he wanted some of the money from his estate to go into a foundation or organization to support people who wanted to get an education. He wanted to help others who were less fortunate. Randy was guiding Marcia from the other side in a variety of ways. He even put in his own two cents about the ceremony, sharing that he would prefer to have candles lit and have everyone participate in the reading of a poem. A couple days later, Randy guided me to the perfect poem to fulfill his wishes.

As you can imagine, a situation like this is not easy. There can be feelings of blame and judgment from everyone involved; yet that didn't stop Marcia from being the loving, benevolent woman that she is. Despite feeling indescribable pain in her heart, she stood up in support of her family and friends with absolute unconditional love. I will remember Marcia's courage and actions forever.

Marcia's grace and presence are undeniable, but that doesn't mean she didn't have her share of anger, sadness, and regret. But with the unconditional love that was within her, she chose each and every day to push through the pain and guilt and be who she truly is: a messenger and believer in love. With the help and support of Randy, her heart is healing . . . one day at a time. The greatest thing is that Marcia sees purpose and value in it all, and she truly believes that everything, including suicide, happens for a reason. To quote from the last part of Randy's celebration of life,

> One thing I believe that most of us can agree on is the fact that there are blessings in this terrible tragedy. The importance of connection, communication, support, and loving yourself. These are gifts that Randy leaves with us all . . . to learn, to grow, and to heal from. And now, he soars with the angels.

True love, regardless of how someone passes, never ends—it just changes form.

What Happens When Someone Commits Suicide

Souls that have passed from suicide typically cross over the same way others do. The only difference is that they often spend more time in a healing space, as I like to call it. In this place, the departed loved one can help those who are left in the physical world to heal, as well as resolve some of the pain that caused them to end their life. The amount of time spent in this healing space is different for everyone, and it is based on personal life experiences.

The healing space has been described to me as a place of pure love and light. There are spiritual teachers, guides, and angels infusing your soul with love. It is a place of reflection and learning how and why things happened the way they did. It can also be a place of forgiveness, which is the ultimate healing.

Spirits go to the healing place once they have moved through their life review. I believe while in this healing space, it isn't about judging right and wrong. It is about understanding and integrating how you have expanded.

You can communicate with someone who died through suicide exactly the same way you would communicate with any other loved one who has passed on. I think that oftentimes there is so much surprise, anger, and guilt about the death that it can feel harder to connect with them. But they still want to keep in touch, and they still love you. They just didn't love themselves enough at the time to see through the pain to that love. And you must reach a place of peace and understanding that allows your vibration to support that connection and communication with them as well.

I share this poem as a reminder for us all. If you have walked the journey of suicide, you know that everyone affected is looking for answers to a long list of tough and troubling questions. My intention and hope in sharing this are that it removes some of the questions and assists in reestablishing your connection to your loved one once more.

Responsibility

I have a responsibility to those I love . . .
to be loving, patient, considerate, and kind;
to be loyal, respectful, and honest;
to be appreciative, encouraging, and comforting;

to share myself and care for myself
To be the best possible "ME".
BUT
I am not responsible for them . . .
not for their achievements, successes, or triumphs;
not for their joy, gratification, or fulfillment;
not for their defeats, failures, or disappointments;
not for their thoughts, choices, or mistakes.
And NOT for their death.
For had I been responsible this death would not have
occurred.

—Anonymous

6
Things That Go Bump in the Night

● ● ● ● ● ● ● ● ● ● ● ● ● ● ● ● ● ● ● ●

The wound is the place where the Light enters you.

—Rumi

When we are younger, sometimes the paranormal is scary. Not because it truly is, but because we don't understand it. Well, truth be told, people who are older have the same experiences; they often just have a little less fear of the ghost in the closet or the boogeyman. Sometimes fear manifests because we don't know or understand what is happening. Or sometimes it is because we don't know how to discern the different energies. Discernment is an important part of developing your intuition and learning to tap into the energy of love—which is who we truly are.

When I was nineteen, my mom's cousin-in-law, Shelly, invited me to come to her house for a week to attend her wedding. Then while she honeymooned for a few days, I would stay and watch her eight-year-old son, Mitch. Mitch's dad had died about seven years earlier, and his mom was getting remarried.

Now, I wasn't the babysitting kind of girl, and I was a little nervous about going. But I focused on the adventure of it being my six-month-old son's first airplane trip. It was to be our first vacation, and I was excited!

When we arrived, a lady in a convertible Jeep picked us up from the airport. As I got in, I realized there wasn't a seat belt for my son's car seat. That should have been my first clue of the danger that was yet to come, but I was so happy to be away from the sadness and pain of my own life at the time that I just ignored it. I jumped in, and we headed off to Shelly's, with Crew resting on my lap.

I'd come a couple days before the wedding to help get everything ready, and we weren't the only ones. Upon arriving at Shelly's house, I found it was mass chaos. As soon as I walked into that little two-bedroom condo, I started second-guessing my decision. There were people everywhere, drinking and smoking like crazy. Part of that could have been out of nervousness or celebration, but the addiction energy was everywhere. I knew this because I'd just escaped my own home environment of living with an alcoholic boyfriend and being surrounded by addicts in my life.

Unfortunately, my addiction wasn't alcohol or nicotine, but food. I say unfortunately because there was none of that to be found. And no car to go get any, either. Luckily, my son had formula or we both might have starved those first couple days. I couldn't wait to get to the wedding day to get it done and over with so that everyone could just leave and I could finally breathe. I mean, I was used to chaos, but this was over the top. I said to myself several times, "and I thought my life was dysfunctional!"

I helped with all the final preparations, and once the wedding was over, everyone was off and I felt free. Yay! It was just me, Crew, and Mitch in a cute little condo. A far cry from the shack I was living in at the time. I felt as though I was kind of playing house. I fantasized about what it would be like to live in a "real" house, with neighbors and sidewalks instead of the dead-end dirt road, and life, I was living. I was happy to be there, just me and the kids . . . until it got dark.

That night, while I was downstairs getting Mitch ready for bed, I heard some noises in the other room. Strange noises. It sounded like people were talking, but I couldn't tell what they were saying. I could just hear the dark, low, creepy tones, and it freaked me out. I also heard what sounded like newspapers rustling around. I went into the area where I'd heard the noises, by the closet, but I couldn't see anything. However, I sure could hear and feel it.

I was so scared by this point that I grabbed Mitch and Crew and ran up those stairs faster than lightning. My heart was racing a thousand beats a minute, and my palms were so sweaty I could barely keep my grip on my baby as I ran. Once we were up there, the noises got louder. I didn't know what to do.

I took the kids, who were both crying by now, as they could see the panic in my face and the fear in my body, and we sat on the couch and waited. Waited for what, I didn't know. I said a prayer and asked that any energy that was not for our highest good leave immediately. I invoked Archangel Michael to protect us, but it felt like it didn't work. I was still hearing the clanging and deep whispers coming from downstairs.

It was then that I began to feel a different energy around me. I couldn't discern who or what it was; I just knew that this energy felt distinctly different than what I had felt downstairs. I was so scared, though, I didn't take the time to even notice how or why it felt different.

I was completely freaked out, so I called my mom, who was over 500 miles way. I was just sobbing. I was supposed to be the responsible one. I was the parent, the grown-up. But I sure wasn't feeling like much of a grown-up at that point. My mom reiterated the importance of asking for protection and help, which I did several more times. She then reminded me that Shelly was a drug addict, and that the energy I was feeling downstairs was likely the negative energies associated with her. I didn't know if hearing that explanation made me feel better or worse. My mom couldn't do anything to help me; there was no one else to call, and no place else to go. The only place I could go was within.

My mom stayed on the phone with me for at least an hour or so that evening. I stayed up the entire night, too afraid to fall asleep. I lay on the couch with the two boys right on top of me, listening to them breathing in and out. It was like that was my meditation. I focused on their breath, just waiting for the sun to rise and the darkness to be over.

Once the sun came up, I felt safer, more at peace. I went for a walk and tried to clear that experience. I spoke with my mom later that day, and she tried to help me settle down. She reminded me that Mitch's dad had passed and that he had loved his son dearly, and she suggested that I ask him for help that night if I began to feel the same energies. His son was only six months old when he'd died. They were even named after each other, so it was likely that he was a guide for his son as well. He would surely be watching over Mitch Jr.

As day turned to dusk, the fear of going through another night like the last started to creep in. Mitch's bedroom was downstairs, and there were things he needed from that room. So, I got really brave. I grabbed the fire poker, ran downstairs, got what I needed for Mitch for school, and ran back upstairs. He never asked me why I flew up those stairs that day, and I never talked about it with him. There was an unspoken under-standing between us; we'd both felt something. We agreed, silently, to ignore it. I never went down there again.

Tonight, I decided, I was going to take control. I said a prayer of protection right as it got dark. I asked Mitch's dad to protect us too from anything negative, seen or unseen. I asked him to help me release the fear and to feel safe again. Almost immediately, I felt the knot release from my stomach. I felt at ease, as though it was OK. I still heard the noises, but it felt as though they couldn't touch me, like I was completely protected. I wasn't going to push my luck and go downstairs, but I felt safe enough to be upstairs with the boys. We made beds on the couch, and we camped out there the rest of the week. I couldn't explain why I felt OK, except to say that there was this loving presence that I could feel was Mitch's dad. I believe he came immediately to protect us. His love kept us safe.

I was puzzled, though. Why did he not come the first night, when I so desperately asked for help . . . when I was experiencing such deep fear? What I know now is that first night, when I was in so much fear, I couldn't discern his energy. I had mistaken the negative energy I felt downstairs for the loving energy of Mitch's dad that surrounded me upstairs. At that moment, I was in absolute fear mode. I wasn't able to see clearly and really tune into what was actually around me because of the experience I had previously had.

I realized then how fear can create so many illusions in our lives. My illusion was that I was alone, with no help or support. The fear had taken over, and once that happened, I could only see what I had experienced in the past. I was stuck!

I learned too how important it is to be present in the moment. Had I been present, I would have sensed the difference in the energy. Once I was able to be present, calm, and focused with my own energy, I was absolutely able to discern the change. I could then feel the presence of love and allow that loving support of Archangel Michael and Mitch's dad in. Immediately upon doing this, I felt peace.

Even if we aren't aware that love is there, it is, and it will continue to be until we can see and feel it again. This was one of my early experiences into how important it is to free oneself from the grip that fear can have on you and your ability to feel the support that is all around you. The presence of our deceased loved ones comes to us in small and subtle ways. To tune into that new language of love, we must quiet our mind and be open to new feelings, impressions, and emotions.

By this point, I'd come a long way from the scared girl I was in Yellowstone—but I still had work to do. My mistaking Mitch's dad's energy for something else showed me this. Thankfully, Spirit is patient, and we have lots of opportunities to keep learning about life and love. . . . And the journey continues.

Love Will Build the Bridge

It's not very becoming, but a lot of people in this world hold on to grudges. What happens when the grudge-holder passes? Does that ill will go with them, or are negative vibes sent back from the spirit world? Is that what a haunting is? People might wonder.

Typically, after someone passes, they understand their life experiences better; therefore, any grudge they may have held in life would be gone in the spirit realm. However, if this person were in a particularly low vibrational place, they may hold on to it for a time. As their healing occurs, and as you grow and evolve a bit more, the energy of the grudge would be healed as well. I have had a few spirits share their experiences with this from the other side.

I once did a reading for a woman whose ex-husband absolutely hated her. She had come to me to connect with her father, so when her hostile ex-husband showed up, she was not happy. "I don't want to talk to the SOB," she said. I told her before the reading that I couldn't control who comes through, but she was still shocked when he popped in to say hello.

You see, when he was alive on Earth, they were extremely toxic to each other. He confessed that he made her life hell. He just had so much anger about their divorce and her unwillingness to put up with his verbal abuse. When he appeared this time, he apologized immediately. He acknowledged the pain he had put her through and how his addiction had affected the whole family. He said how sorry he was that she had to go through it all.

I watched her soften within five minutes. Even though she didn't want to talk to him, his words were a soothing balm to a still-angry woman. The pain, the grudge they held against one another even into the afterlife, was healed. Love had softened their hearts

Remember, even those who have passed who are at a lower energy level are still with us in love. There is nothing to fear. It is love that will build the bridge from our world to the spirit world, so stay in the vibration of love as much as possible.

What Are Ghosts?
Are They Something to Fear?

Ghosts are not necessarily evil spirits, contrary to what Hollywood horror movies might suggest. They are just spirits that have passed away and are not ready to go to the light yet. They could be unaware that they have passed, or they could still feel the need to stay close. There are a variety of reasons for why they might stay. Usually it is because they feel they have some kind of unfinished business. If a soul wants to return to Earth to "fix" things or to help people to heal in spirit form, it is up to us to listen so that they don't have to stay here any longer than necessary, and so that they can move on in their new experience.

What about the "bad" people who pass? Do they have more of a will, or a way, to stay behind to haunt us? The simple answer is, no. All of Spirit is created in unconditional love, so there are no "bad" spirits. Therefore, they go to the same place as everyone else. Some might call it heaven, some call it hell. I call it all vibration.

There is higher vibrational space and lower vibrational space in the spirit world just as there is in our earthly world. We have people who are in a higher vibration place; some might call them "good" people. We have others who are in a lower vibrational place; some might call them "bad" people. "Good" and "bad" are human words based on a judgment that doesn't exist in the spirit world. So, if we take judgment out of it, a lower vibrational place is just a place—not good, not bad. It simply is. My experience is if someone was a high vibrational being in the earthly world, they will move to that equivalent in the spirit world. Conversely, those functioning at a lower vibration here would move on to a lower vibrational place.

Does purgatory exist? Or serving penance for wrongdoings that happened in this lifetime? It has never been my experience that there is any type of purgatory or place of penance, even for what you might call the worst people. My experience is one of light and love, growth, awareness, and expansion. Those we might assume go to purgatory receive the same healing energies, love, and support in the spirit world as those who are worshipped as enlightened beings or wise men in the physical world.

As I have mentioned throughout the book, there truly is nothing to fear when connecting with your deceased loved ones. They have moved into a vibrational place that is more aware than when they were here. That doesn't mean that everything is resolved, but the peace of their passing could allow you to release the pain and find peace too.

7
Help from Beyond the Grave

• •

Those we love don't go away. They walk beside us every day.

—Anonymous

I met Melissa at a book signing in Santa Rosa, California. We set up a meeting for the next day so that I could do a private reading with her. As we began the reading, I could feel a tremendous amount of fear and grief around her as she asked about her troubled son. She wanted to know if he was going to be OK.

The answer I received from Spirit was that it was going to be a tough year, but her son's spirit was strong enough to move through it. Although it would be a rocky road, she needed to let him go and have his experiences. Then the healing could occur around the challenges he had created.

One message that really resonated with her was, "His soul is just as strong as yours, and just because you came here first does not mean you know more." She had to begin to trust her son's spirit, and the spirits of those around him. This would be a powerful gift to them both.

Trust was the gift that would eventually come out of that reading, but what happened next was critical to Melissa's healing process. I could feel her mom's presence, so I asked her what her mom's name and birth date were. These are two things that help me tune into the different spirits around people. As I tuned into her mom's energy, I could feel the pressure in my heart and lungs and knew that she had died of lung cancer. As I connected a little deeper with Melissa's mom, she told me about this very special blanket that Melissa had embroidered for her with so much love. She described the blanket having a big butterfly in the center, and on the wings it said: Hope, Faith, and Love. Around the butterfly, she had embroidered all of the names in their family, every single one, right down to the great-grandkids. Melissa's mom loved that blanket and told me how it had carried her through her illness and given her much love and peace during those times. Although Melissa lived across the United States, her mother said she could feel Melissa's love every time the blanket was placed on her. Her mother also shared with me how this blanket had gone with her on her journey from this world to the spirit world and was buried with her physical body.

As I shared these messages from her mother, Melissa's eyes welled up with tears. To know that her mom could feel her love and gratitude on the other side was the greatest gift she could have received. It was exactly the validation the whole family needed. Melissa confirmed that that same butterfly blanket was laid on her mother the morning right before she passed, and before they closed the casket, they put it on her and buried her with it.

As those pieces settled in, an image suddenly came to me and I blurted out, "the ring!" Mom wanted to talk about the ring she had given Melissa. This brought a huge smile to Melissa's face. I could feel that her mother was a smaller woman, and I saw a ring being forced onto a finger that was too big for it.

Her mother was telling me that Melissa was wearing her ring, but that it was too small for her. We both had a good laugh as she showed me her mother's wedding ring on her pinky finger. Melissa had bugged her mother for fourteen years for that ring. When she got engaged, she asked her mom for her old wedding ring, but her mom just wouldn't give it up. It turned into a game between the two of them. "Do you have a gift for me?" Melissa would ask, and again and again her mom would deny her. It wasn't until her mom fell ill that she handed it over, with love in her heart. Melissa cherishes those memories and that very special ring, to this day.

As our reading continued, Melissa's mom wanted to make sure that Melissa and her brother knew how much she appreciated them. She thanked them both for their long trips to New York to help their father and said that had they not come, their father would not have been able to do it, physically or emotionally. She was so grateful to them for taking care of her through her transition and recognized what a sacrifice it was to them as well. She said, "You know as well as I do that without you, Dad would have had to put me in hospice." He simply was not able to take care of her. But through her children's love, she was able to stay at home and live out her last days surrounded by the ones she loved.

Melissa cried as her mom's acknowledgment sank in. The tears that fell from her eyes were tears of acceptance and validation that someone she loved was nearby and speaking directly to her. It was beautiful to witness.

This was the beginning of Melissa's healing journey. She was so excited about the messages she received from her mom that she had her dad and brother set up an appointment with me. Over the next few months I connected with each of them and brought her mom through to them as well so they could all connect with her. It was a joy to feel that same sense of appreciation and closure from each of them.

It was a few months later when I heard from Melissa again. This time she sent me an email reminding me that in all three separate telephone readings, her mother had come through with a grave concern about a young man sixteen to twenty years old. In the three readings (for her, her brother, and her dad, spanning different states and times), Melissa's mom had mentioned that she was spending all of her time with a young family member who had an addiction problem. At the time, they were all perplexed and couldn't imagine who it could be. It was shortly thereafter that Melissa's son came clean about his meth addiction. He was seventeen at the time, and his grandmother had been keeping a watchful eye on him and guiding his very strong spirit. After a stint at juvenile hall and rehab, her son got clean. At the time of this writing, he has been clean for thirteen months!

In this instance, the gifts from Melissa's mother came in two different stages. The more immediate gift happened when the family received gratitude for their loving actions toward their mother in her final days. This brought comfort and aided in the grieving and healing process for everyone. Their vibration was raised and the joy and the connection they felt with their mother grew stronger even after her death.

The second gift took a little longer to unfold. As time passed, they were able to understand more of what was happening in their physical world, and they could appreciate an even more powerful gift from their mother. For it was the heart connection that lived on between this family that allowed Melissa's son to be watched over and guided long before he was able to recognize and openly receive that love and support in the "real" world. It was the trust that grew stronger between Melissa and her deceased mother that allowed her to have the strength to believe in her son's spirit even in the most troubling of times.

A Life-Saving Message from Beyond

Murder is always a hard topic to speak about, let alone write about. In my experience, it is surrounded by anger, blame, and pain, which can make it very difficult to feel the love from the other side. Such was the case for the following family.

I met this family shortly after their twenty-four-year-old son David was shot and killed. David's mother Karen, his sister Carrie, his cousin Cindy, and his Aunt Denise came to a class I was teaching on death and dying at a local library to learn more about the death process and what happens after we die.

Throughout the workshop, each family member was having her own experience—and difficulties—with some of the class topics. During one exercise, I asked students to give up things that were important to them, as people are often forced to do when they are dying. It was the process of walking through their own death that was particularly painful for Karen—and understandably so. As she struggled to complete the exercise, every time something was heart-wrenching for her to give up, she would see a bright light behind me as I was teaching. She hoped it was her son. Seeing this light brought her calmness as she recognized that he was possibly still with her.

At another point in the class, during a somber moment, everyone was quiet and Carrie suddenly yelled out *Ahhhhh!* really loud. She'd felt a wet willy, which she tried to blame on her cousin sitting next to her. But they both knew. It was her brother giving his sister a little extra love! He was there with them that evening, trying to lighten up a difficult situation. That was his personality on Earth: fun loving and silly. He was always playing jokes and supporting those he cared about.

After the class was over and everyone else had left, I asked the family to stay behind for a minute because I could sense how incredible and strong David's presence was in their lives. Throughout the class I could see his bright light around them, I could hear his gregarious laugh, and I could see his silliness as he gave his sister the wet willy. I explained to them the different levels of vibration and how he had to lower his vibration and they had to raise theirs to be able to connect and receive messages, dreams, or communication. I told them that I felt as though their son was a teacher and chose to be very present on Earth to show them how to communicate with him. I also confirmed that he had been standing behind me during most of the class, which was a great validation to his mom. She missed him terribly and wanted nothing more than to see and feel him again.

David was a motorcycle enthusiast, and I could feel his love for his bikes was outweighed only by his love for his family and friends. He was a big teddy bear. Tough, athletic biker dude with tattoos on the outside, but a teddy bear on the inside— he'd do anything for anyone and had big love for his family and friends.

As I shared more with the family, I could see the aha moments coming together for them. Things were starting to make sense. David had been doing lots of things to try to communicate with them: leaving feathers for them to find; opening things, such as the refrigerator, the dryer, and drawers; moving objects right in front of them; and visiting them in their dreams and visualizations. David even scolded his mom a little bit by having me tell her that he was trying to speak to her but she just kept pushing him off.

After this experience, Karen felt an overwhelming sense of peace for the first time since David had died. She began to slowly feel more and more connected and understanding of his gifts as their angel. The family, with David's nudging, decided they wanted to learn more about how to communicate with him, and over the next several years I got to know them very well through classes, healing retreats, and workshops. I got to know David very well too, as he was always outspoken . . . always.

A few years later, I was conducting a gallery reading at my healing center. I currently hold gallery readings once a month and give people the opportunity to come and ask questions, and I do live mini-readings. This particular evening, David showed up with his aunt Denise and cousin Cindy. Now, David was a special guy, and although he was in spirit, he always had a big, strong, intense energy. Throughout the evening, I felt him standing over me, and he insisted that he had a message for his family and he wanted to make sure they heard it. I could feel him pushing, and I pushed back a little. "Wait in line, David," is what I was telepathically saying to him as I tried to be present to the other people and spirits in the room. It was not an easy task.

Typically when I do a mediumship reading, I hear the messages of deceased loved ones, I get impressions of them in my mind, or I see them. However, on this occasion, David chose to literally come through me. He had a very important and very intense message that he had to share with his dad, and this time he wasn't going to leave it up to me. This message was so urgent and so powerful that he literally came into my body. My mannerisms changed, my speech changed, my body position changed, even my facial features changed. I felt as though I had gained a hundred pounds and grown ten inches. Those in attendance were shocked, as was I. Not because it happened, but because typically David just gives me a strong message to share with his family. He comes across BIG and strong and that is enough. But this time, his message was bigger than me. With him being on the other side, he would know that although I choose not to practice, I am a trained trans channel as well. So, this experience, although not one I practice regularly, was not new for me.

His message was clear and to the point. David told his dad that he needed to forgive and pull his head out of his ass. David said that he was creating physical disease from his buried pain, and if he did not attend to the pain, it would kill him. He was not messing around.

The love that David has for his family has been so evident over the years. And persistent people become persistent spirits. If someone can't or won't let the love in, a spirit can choose to get their attention in other ways, as David did.

I found out after the reading that David's dad had been struggling more than I had realized. He was an alcoholic, and his drinking problem had been exacerbated by David's death. He was also dealing with some very serious health issues on top of that. Fortunately, David's message of love scared his dad enough to do something different. Shortly after that experience, he went to the doctor, something he hadn't done for years. His grief and emotional pain had taken a toll on him mentally and physically, manifesting in a life-threatening heart condition, along with a variety of other illnesses. Once he heard David Jr.'s straightforward message, he started taking better care of himself, taking medication, and attending private sessions to help heal and deal with his pain and grief.

David's dad knows his son's insistence from the afterlife had a huge role in him stepping forward to begin his healing. Although he can't really explain the depth of his experiences, he knows the love and peace he feels can only come from one person—his son.

8

Is Reincarnation Real?

- -

Love never ends. As for prophecies, they will pass away; as
for tongues, they will cease; as for knowledge, it will pass
away. For we know in part and we prophesy in part, but
when the perfect comes, the partial will pass away. When I
was a child, I spoke like a child, I thought like a child, I rea-
soned like a child. When I became a man, I gave up child-
ish ways. For now we see in a mirror dimly, but then face
to face. Now I know in part; then I shall know fully, even as
I have been fully known.

—1 Corinthians 13:8–13

It's not very often that I get to do a reading just for fun. However, several years ago, a client came to me just to see what
loved ones were connected to her. Not for closure, but for validation of information she had learned while researching her
family's history.

When this particular woman walked in, she walked in with
a "gang." She had all kinds of deceased loved ones around
her. Between the ones I could see and the ones I could feel,
I believe we brought through eighteen different family members, going as far back as six generations.

It was amazing—with each person who came through, I'd
give her details about that person, and she'd know who it was.

We're not just talking grandparents. We are talking great-great-great-great-great-grandparents and uncles and such.

I remember two men who came through together in particular. They were brothers. As I began to tune into their energy, I heard the song "I've Been Working on the Railroad" in my head. They communicated to me that they had made their living by working on the railroad. As I shared this with my client, a huge grin appeared on her face. I continued to share the vision I had of them arm in arm, wearing overalls and with filthy hands. They also shared their last name and showed me the number 1826, which we believed to be the year of the younger brother's birth.

This client was so excited because she was able to receive validation that her genealogy, which she had spent endless hours on, was correct (her great-great-grandfather and uncle had been railroad workers in the early nineteenth century). Throughout the session, information poured out through me about one relative and then another and then another. This lady had researched back so many generations that she knew a lot of details of the spirits who appeared that day. That made it fun for me, too.

As a medium, I have noticed that oftentimes people get what I call "psychic amnesia." They forget their own family members' names, dates of birth, where they live, etc., because in that moment they are either very excited or very nervous. For both of us that day, it was like we got to put the pieces of the puzzle together. Even though she never knew these men, not consciously anyway, the love connection had traveled through the generations. It had guided her to do this genealogy, to tell their story, and then to connect with me so she could validate it.

This client's connection to one of the railroad brothers was particularly interesting, and it made me wonder if he could possibly be her own soul inhabiting a different body in the past. In *Healing Ancestral Karma,* Dr. Steven Farmer suggests this is possible. He believes that the deceased loved ones you're connecting with quite often appear to offer you healing, and in return they receive karmic healing through your acknowledgment of them. This helps them through their own soul's evolution in the afterlife.

We have soul families. The members return to Earth time and time again to learn and evolve and expand. So, wouldn't it make sense then that if you were Jack in 1845, you could come back as your own great-great-great-granddaughter in 1999? The two of you, connected as family through your DNA and through your love, could be one and the same soul. Now, that really would show us that love never ends, wouldn't it? It just keeps cycling in and out and in and out.

This seems like a good opportunity to explain my understanding of reincarnation. I believe that our *soul* exists in the spirit world. It will always be in the spirit world. Our *spirit,* an aspect or part of our soul, will incarnate into a physical body and experience a particular lifetime. While our spirit is in a physical body, it always remains connected to our soul in the spirit world.

Some people refer to a "higher self." For me, the higher self is the soul. Now, when our physical body dies, our spirit returns to the spirit world and rejoins with our soul. Our soul then has all of our lifetimes of experience to expand and grow from the hundreds or perhaps even thousands of lifetimes that we have incarnated.

The communication we receive from our ancestors can help us with our healing, or their healing, or, in the case of the woman's story earlier, it can validate our beliefs and bring us joy as we connect with them in our physical lives. And it is

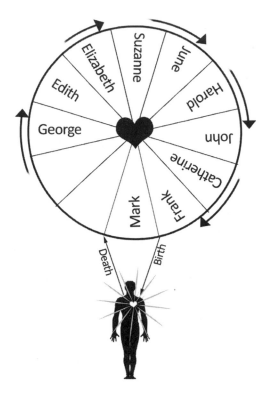

The circle represents your soul (nonphysical).

The heart represents your spirit, the connection to the nonphysical (your soul).

The names within the circle represent each physical incarnation (lifetime) you have lived. Each name is an aspect, a part of your soul. The empty aspects are incarnations (lives) still to come.

There could be hundreds of incarnations.

When you are born, an aspect of your soul incarnates into the body (known as Mark in this description). When Mark dies, he reemerges back into the nonphysical (his soul).

The the cycle repeats itself.

So Mark was Frank in a previous life and before that was Catherine, and before that John, etc.

All of the time, the soul is intact, and the spirit that has incarnated (Mark) is always connected to the nonphysical (his soul).

possible that the individuals we are especially drawn to from our past may in fact be an aspect of our very own soul. Surely there could be no greater confirmation that our love and spirit live on forever!

Once you return to Spirit, you have knowledge of all that you are and all that you have been. You may not choose to focus on it, but you are aware of all aspects of your soul or all expressions of your divine light. Once in heaven, you are no longer a person with a name. You are a soul, a vibrational, infinite being. If you choose to reincarnate quickly, you will still have the ability to communicate with those left behind because your soul will still be intact.

I don't believe there is an average amount of time that it takes to incarnate. Each soul has its own journey, and so there is not a way to measure the amount of time it takes for one to complete it. My sense is that once one aspect of expansion has been completed, a soul will incarnate to create more opportunities for expansion. When we die, we may be in the spirit world for ten years or a hundred years. When we are complete with that aspect of expansion, that's the point at which we can return again. We could also go to other realms to expand. This Earth is not our only choice, though many souls do choose to return here. We come here to experience expansion and contrast. That is what the physical world can offer in ways that the spirit world does not.

Reincarnation then makes complete sense to me. I personally have had memories of several past lives, some very positive and some extremely traumatic and painful. I was a cowboy in the late 1800s during a life that was full of adventure; however, I was persecuted and hung for my spiritual beliefs in another incarnation that had much fear and struggle associated with it. For me there is no question that reincarnation exists. I find it impossible to believe in the old adage, "You only live once." It simply does not fit for me.

Karma, on the other hand, is a little bit tricky. Karma, simply put, is the cause and effect result of our own past actions and present activities. I absolutely believe in karma as well. At the age of eight, I created what I thought was my own motto: "What goes around comes around." I came to find out it was already a very popular saying. Nevertheless, it was one that I completely embraced. I said it all the time. I knew it. I believed it. It was my truth. As soon as I was old enough to have a checking account, I had it printed on my checks as a statement of my truth and as a constant reminder to myself. But along with this belief, I live life from another concept that rings true for me as well: We are responsible for our own pleasure and pain. We create our own heaven and our own hell—right here on Earth. We are the creators of our reality.

Many people believe that karma in the present affects one's future in the current life, as well as the nature and quality of future lives. That may be true. However, how much focus we put on karma can create its own challenges in the lifetime we are living now. Some people believe you have karmic debt from other lifetimes that must be balanced out; others believe karma exists to bring balance within each lifetime. This is a question I believe you must ask yourself, as these can be difficult concepts to process as we experience our opportunities for growth in this physical world. I personally tend to just listen to my heart and trust that everything is happening in divine order, for my highest good, at any given time. I don't mentally "keep score." As long as I honor others and myself in a loving way throughout the variety of life experiences I have, then I am honoring any karmic debt I may have.

If we allow it, these concepts can become a great source of fear and resistance to many of us. And that can only serve to lower your current vibration and limit your ability to learn and expand as you intended in this lifetime. It is not necessary to understand what lessons your soul has chosen to learn in this lifetime. I don't even feel it is absolutely necessary to make a conscious connection to how current situations may be providing karmic healing for past incarnations or setting up opportunities to expand in the future. I do believe what is most important is to really allow yourself to approach your experiences in this lifetime as always having a purpose and to always give yourself an opportunity to be present in the now.

We've covered some exercises already that allow you to strengthen your connection to the spirit world, and these are the same tools that will allow you to gain the most from your experiences in this lifetime: Work at staying present and aware; broaden your perspective that love is the guiding force for all your soul experiences; and trust that this love never ends . . . in any lifetime!

We do not need to fear what our future soul lessons may have in store for us. We are divinely prepared for each and every journey we begin. When thinking about past or future lives, some people wonder if we could come back as a dog or another animal. Humans are constantly evolving, as are animals. But animals come in with a different intention than humans. This is not to say that animals are a lower vibration; in fact, quite the opposite. Animals already know that they are love, and they just allow it. Humans, on the other hand, explore more contrast in order to expand and grow. Therefore, a human would not come back as an animal, and an animal would not come back as a human. We'll learn more about messages from pets in the next chapter. But whatever path your spiritual journey takes you on—for whatever number of lifetimes this may represent—we are all here to fulfill one mission: to grow and expand in unconditional love for ourselves and all beings around us.

9
What About Pets?

· · · · · · · · · · · · · ·

Thus all things are but alter'd, nothing dies;
And here and there the unbodied spirit flies
—Ovid, *Metamorphoses*

When it comes to the loss of a loved one, you may be surprised to know that very often the deepest loss I see is that of a beloved pet. I hope you'll be relieved to know that many deceased loved ones report that they are with their animals once they return home or their pets were there to greet them when they transitioned. I've done readings where all kinds of animals come through, too: horses, dogs, cats, goats, hamsters—even a goldfish. The messages they share are of absolute, unconditional love. Our beloved pets go to the same place as we do, so they are absolutely waiting for you on the other side.

It is such a comfort for people to hear that their cherished pets are with them once they pass, hanging out like usual. It is even more encouraging to learn that when they pass, their pets will be there to welcome them home. Unfortunately, the depth of pain and grief people experience with the loss of a pet is often devastating. It can be even more difficult for some than losing a friend or family member because, although we love our family and friends, for many, there is no greater love than the unconditional love of a pet.

Most of the time, when people come in for a reading, they are looking to connect with their human deceased loved ones. That was not the case with one client, Valerie. I had never met Valerie before, and she had driven from another state to have the reading done in person. When she walked in, I could feel her overwhelming grief. She was absolutely heartbroken. As we sat down and began to chat, her dog Trixie began to allow me to experience, in my body, what it felt like for her in the last moments of her life.

When we think of the last moments of a life, our fear often goes to what they were experiencing physically: How much pain were they in? Could we have done anything different to help? Trixie didn't want to focus on that; she wanted to show me something different. First, Trixie showed me that this was a decision that Valerie had to make. However, Valerie's decision continued to haunt her every second of the day. The guilt and the pain tormented her every moment. For Trixie, that decision was necessary to free her from her physical form. Trixie allowed me to experience her feeling of freedom and absolute joy! She appeared excited and playful, full of light, love, joy, and life!

Trixie shared with me that she did not want to be in her body any longer, and that Valerie had saved her! In Valerie's eyes, making the tough decision to put Trixie down meant she had killed her dog. What I shared with Valerie is that Trixie was grateful and free and that she would have never felt this freedom in her physical body again. Trixie wanted Valerie to get out more, to go for walks again, and to start living life again. She told Valerie she would never leave her side, just like when she was alive, and she said that if Valerie would go for walks, Trixie would guide her. The depth of their love was truly astounding.

As I shared all this with Valerie, she just cried. She was happy for Trixie yet still sad for herself. The heaviness that she walked into the room with, however, had been replaced with some peace in her heart. She had done the right thing! Trixie was free, and they would always be together—especially on their favorite walks. Valerie left our session with a lightness, a knowing, and a restored sense of faith that their love and strong bond had continued beyond this physical world. The healing had begun.

It's especially important for people with pets that have passed to acknowledge their connection. As you can see from Valerie's story, just the realization that pets are still with us can pull you out of your pain. Or, as is the case in the next story, it can completely release you from your doubt and fear.

I have a very dear longtime client, Monica, who had an adorable little dog named Lily Bean. She was the light of Monica's life. One night, Monica took Lily Bean for a walk and gave her a little treat of ice cream afterward. Everything seemed fine, but the next morning Lily Bean got sick and Monica knew something was seriously wrong. She rushed Lily Bean to the vet, and that was where she discovered her beloved pet had a tumor in her belly. Just hours later, Lily Bean passed away.

Monica sank into a dark, painful canyon where she was unable to feel the presence of Lily, her angels, or even God. She was angry, stunned, and confused. She felt abandoned and alone. You see, Monica had spent her entire adult life creating a loving connection with Spirit that was beyond her wildest dreams. But in the midst of her grief, she began to doubt all that she had learned and experienced. She began to question everything she knew. She asked herself, "What if this is all BS, and we're just making up all of this life after death stuff to make it easier to cope with death? What if everything I have ever thought, believed, experienced, or imagined was just a bunch of crap and we are really just alone on this crazy planet?" After a few days of sitting home alone and grieving, Monica realized how Lily's death was affecting her body, mind, and spirit in such a dark and unhealthy way, and she contacted me.

As soon as Monica walked into my office, I could see and feel Lily; but more than that, I could feel how very depressed, angry, and full of doubt Monica was. So much so that she was thinking of ending her career as a spiritual teacher and workshop leader. After all, she felt like there was no way she was going to be able to teach others about what she now feared might not even exist. She was in tremendous pain, and initially all I could do was hug her.

We ended our embrace, and then I started the reading. I could see Lily was an energetic dog with a really sweet, fun-loving personality. She came right through as if she were with us in physical form. I described Lily to Monica and told her I saw her running through tons of green grass, happy and free. But there was something else. Little Lily had this funny sideways gallop. At first, I didn't know how to explain it; but as I began to describe what Lily was doing, Monica broke down in tears.

"That's my Lily Bean," she cried out. She realized then that she was really here with us at that moment. All those doubts and fears were just feelings—and the emotions faded away. But that wasn't all. Lily had some important messages to get to Monica.

Lily told me that she still had a very important role to play in Monica's life and that she would be helping her enhance her spiritual healing gifts. Lily would be working with Monica from the other side now, which would help her to discover an even deeper connection with Spirit and trust in her intuition even more. Lily would now be an animal guide of Monica's.

While we can feel desperate loss over the passing of an animal friend, from my understanding there is no difference between an animal's passing and a person's passing. Just as it is when we humans transition, there is no pain at the moment of death for animals either—nor are they alone. If your dear dog, cat, or any other kind of animal transitions before you, never worry that they are there alone; they have already rejoined family members who have gone before them, who love them as much as you do.

Our pets watch after us from the other side and continue to help us with their unconditional support and love, just as they did in life.

Within days of my conversation with Monica, her heart and intuitive abilities began to expand like never before. Lily's spirit had become an important guide during Monica's daily tasks in life as well as in her work with others. Monica has expressed her gratitude for the messages Lily was able to pass on through me, and she's still receiving guidance from her dear pet.

Our beloved pets not only show us unconditional love, they also help us to lighten up, as my new friend Max made evident last month.

Every month I hold an event at my healing center in Glendale, Arizona, called Spirit Talk. During this event, people have an opportunity to ask me a question on any subject matter and I tune into the spirit world and answer according to my guidance. It's kind of a Q&A for the soul. There are always a wide variety of questions, and it is always a learning experience for everyone, myself included. This particular session was especially entertaining, though!

At my most recent Spirit Talk, a man named Josh waited patiently until nearly the end of the event to ask his question. When it was his turn, he didn't have a specific question—he wanted Spirit to guide the reading and asked me to tune into his energy and see what I felt. Immediately I could feel a sense of loss, and I knew that he had lost his best friend. As I tuned in more deeply, I could feel the presence of Max. But Max was no ordinary best friend. He was a furry, four-legged, feline companion. They were best buddies who were still very much connected.

Max shared with me that he had died recently, which was confirmed through the tears in Josh's eyes as we talked about him a bit. Max was a funny one. He had a great sense of humor, which I didn't know cats even had; but boy, Max sure did. Most of the time when an animal comes through to me, it is through feeling and vibration, but not with Max. No, he came through verbally, with Morgan Freeman's voice (think of God in the movie *Bruce Almighty*). It was hilarious.

As Max came through, he mostly wanted Josh to know how important he was to him and how loved he had always felt. He acknowledged that Josh had treated him like one of his children, loving him unconditionally, even spoiling him. I remember Max impressed a feeling of acceptance and love that was not of this physical world. This was a spiritual, soulful connection. It was amazing to be a witness to the energy between the two of them.

Before the energy dissipated, the big cat energy that I had come to know as Max left Josh with an amazing gift. Max reminded Josh of a way to know when he was still around. He would feel him! Max went on to share with me that he loved to polish Josh's shoes. As Max put it, it was a constant practice he had enjoyed during his physical presence. He would go back and forth and back and forth, and rub himself on Josh's leg. But the human joke was that all the while, he was really keeping Josh's shoes polished in the process. With this reminder, Max left Josh with a lighthearted humorous image to hold on to, one that would heal his pain and turn his sadness into hope that Max would continue to be with him going forward. Josh was reminded, through his cat Max, that their love had not ended.

10
Setting Boundaries and Holding Your Energy

● ●

Death is no more than passing from one room into another.
But there's a difference for me, you know. Because in that
other room I shall be able to see.

—Helen Keller

Up to this point, we've assumed that all communication with
our deceased loved ones is good. But what if you're concerned
that they're too involved in your life here on Earth? Or what
if you're too attached to them, and they're ready to move on
to their next phase in spirit? That's where setting boundaries
comes in.

About ten years ago, I had a real estate agent call me to clear
a house that had spirit activity. He didn't understand what was
happening or even believe that it was Spirit. But he knew something didn't feel right and that there was something holding
him back from selling it. When people would come to the showing, odd things would happen. Doors would close, lights would
turn on, water would begin running in the bathroom. Things
he couldn't explain continued to take place and were imped-
ing the sale of this home. He said he'd already lost buyers three

times because people were freaked out. So he asked me to come over ASAP and "do whatever you need to do to get whatever it is out, so I can make this sale." (Note the energy in those words—are they loving or fearful?)

When I walked into the home, I didn't feel at all what everyone else had felt; I sensed sadness, pain, and even resentment. As I walked through the house, which still had a collection of odds and ends—furniture, tools, and such—scattered throughout, I learned the story of Vince.

Vince had lived and died in this home. In life he had worked hard for everything he had, and he did not want to let it go. He was upset about the way people were handling his things and just throwing them around as if they didn't mean anything, as if they weren't of any value. He hated that all of his stuff was piled up in the garage. He didn't like the way the workers came in and started changing things. He didn't feel respected in his own home. As I shared the insights Vince was giving me with the agent, he just nodded. He knew Vince's history and was amazed. I continued to share that Vince wasn't ready to let go yet, and that no one was listening. That was why he was "haunting" the place. He was trying to get someone's attention.

Now, clearly, Vince was no longer alive, but his spirit was still very much attached to the earthly plane. What Vince needed was love and acknowledgment; it was that simple. As I continued to walk through the home, I saw that Vince was a loner. He didn't have many people in his life. He never really cared for them. He had been hurt by a lot of folks and therefore didn't trust a whole lot. Now, why was this important? Because in the "haunting," his spirit was crying out for freedom from the pain, for a release.

Now it was time to allow that release and shift the energy of fear to love. In this way, I could create the energetic boundary of space needed so that Vince could move on. I walked through the house again, this time with the intent of bringing the vibration of love into my body. I imagined myself channeling love out into the corners of every room. I felt myself vibrating the energy of love, and I held the vision of Vince receiving it. I acknowledged him as I felt his presence, and I validated his need to be heard and respected and loved. I held the vision of him finding his freedom and releasing his own fear so that he could move on. I spent about a half hour or so just radiating that love. And then, all of a sudden, it felt complete. The energy had transmuted, and the house was clear. I finished my visit by invoking Archangel Michael to help maintain the energy of love that had been created. At that point I found the agent outside and told him that it was all clear. Vince's spirit had left, and the house would sell very shortly. His eyebrow raised a bit as if to say, It was that simple? My answer? Yes. Love heals! (And yes, the house sold shortly after the clearing.)

This is just one example. Over the years I have had many appointments to clear houses, offices, cars, properties, and even people from spirits that overstep their bounds. Now, I wouldn't say that I have ever felt scared when clearing a space, but I have certainly witnessed the fear in many of my clients. I believe part of the fear is interpreting the unknown as being negative, as I discussed earlier. But there is another side to this: setting boundaries.

Boundaries are based on love, not fear. Some spirits—especially low vibrational sprits—don't have boundaries. They react just like human beings when it comes to personal space. They do not necessarily mean to harm you, like you might have seen on a TV show or in the movies; they are just misdirecting their energy, and they need to be taught through love. Negative spirits are low vibrational beings that haven't yet accepted love from others or from the healing space; they've chosen to stay in a heavier vibrational space. This could happen for a variety of reasons.

In order to create boundaries, all you need is love. Love is the master healer. It heals everything, including fear. Fear, remember, is a low vibration, while love is a high vibration. Fears brings on more fear. However, if love expands, then fear cannot exist in the presence of love. So the simplest—and sometimes the most challenging—way to clear negative energies is to bring love into the space. Pure, unconditional love.

Think about it this way: The lower the vibration or the darker an energy is, the farther away it is from the highest vibration of love and light. The farther distance a vibration is from love, the more love is needed to raise the vibration. When you then infuse a space, an energy, an entity, or a person with love and light, one of two things happens. Either the energy absorbs the love and the negative vibration is transmuted, or the energy flees, as darkness cannot dwell in love and light.

How do I bring in love and clear the space then, you might wonder. There are several different ways, and no one way is the right way, as long as you bring love to the space, the situation, or the person. Some people are comfortable with prayer. If that feels good to you, I have shared two prayers below that have been very helpful in my life. I also have used the Lord's Prayer from time to time as well. Some people like to use physical tools, such as sage, Nag Champa incense, palo santo, crystals, sacred ritual, or spirit spritzers to help remove negative energy. To me, it isn't about what you are using, it is about the loving energy you are bringing into the space. So, whatever tools feel right to you will work so long as you can release the fear and come from a place of love. If you don't think you are in a place to do that, for whatever reason, then invite someone in—a friend, a minister, a counselor, or a medium who can stand in the space with love—and that will take care of it, too.

Saying the following prayers with love and positive intention is really all that needs to be done. Truthfully, if you just vibrated to the energy of love and intention, you wouldn't even need the words, but the words help fulfill that human part of us that feels the need to "do" something. Again, when saying any prayer or blessing, the key is to infuse your words with love, light, and positive intentions. As you do this, the vibration of love and light transmutes any darkness. And remember, you don't want to just mindlessly repeat a prayer or mantra. You want to feel it. It must be active, or *vibrating.*

Archangel Michael Visualization and Prayer

Each morning, before stepping out of bed, I suggest you do the following visualization along with the invocation of Archangel Michael.

Begin by either lying in bed or sitting up in a comfortable position. Quiet your mind, and visualize a sapphire-blue bubble completely surrounding you. Imagine yourself being completely embraced by this beautiful, brilliant energy.

As you do this, know that this is the energy of Archangel Michael and that you are completely surrounded and protected from negative energies. Release any fear-based thoughts by bringing in the intention of love, and focus on being in the present. This is where Spirit speaks and where you can connect.

As you visualize this protective layer of sapphire blue around you, say the invocation below, or some form of it:

I now invoke the loving blue light of Archangel Michael to surround and protect me. I ask that he bring me courage and strength and protect me from any negative energies, seen or unseen. I ask that the brilliant blue energy of protection be placed above me, below me, and all around me so that only pure love and light that is of the highest good can surround me. And so it is.

Do this exercise not from a place of fear, but from a place of loving-kindness to yourself. It serves not only to protect yourself from negative energies, but also to strengthen and maintain your own personal energy field, continually revitalizing and supporting you throughout the day.

White Light Prayer

My mother taught me a simple version of this prayer when I was a teenager. Throughout the years I have added to it and adjusted it to fit what feels right to me at any given time. You can use this prayer as part of your daily spiritual practice or just when you feel guided. Many of my clients use it when they are struggling with fear, as a way of reaching out and seeking help from the spirit world. The prayer can be said in a formal setting, on hands and knees in your home or in a church, or it can be telepathically sent (or anywhere in between). There really is not a right time or place to use this prayer. The most important thing to remember is to use this prayer as you are guided to. Your intuition will not let you down. You will know!

I call on the archangels, ascended masters, spirit guides, helpers, and deceased loved ones to surround me in white light and to guide me and protect me. I ask that you work through me to clear any anger, fear, judgment, or guilt. I ask that my spirit be an open and clear channel of love to provide the highest good for all concerned. Anything that is not of love and light, I send love. Thank you for surrounding me. I am filled with the spirit of love and light, always and in all ways. And so it is.

Where Have They Gone?

Our loved ones can be with us years after they pass, but they will continue to grow and learn in the spirit world, and sometimes they may need to move on. Fortunately, they can connect with us whenever they wish. But the frequency of their visits might decline over time.

You'll notice that as you become more intuitive, you'll find some deceased loved ones really are closer, and some will move on. It makes no difference how long they have been gone, either. Sometimes people will think that because one spirit passed away twenty years ago and another passed away two years ago, the one that passed more recently should stick around longer. That is not necessarily the case. It really depends on each individual spirit's journey, not on time. Remember, there is no time in the spirit world.

If you were married to someone or were in a long-term loving relationship prior to death, I wouldn't say the marriage continues, as marriage is a human experience. But the heart connection, the love, continues on. Over and over, many times, with many different beings, throughout lifetimes.

Why is it that some people communicate with their loved ones when they pass and others don't? How do spirits choose whom they will relay messages through? Unfortunately, I don't really understand this myself. It is possible spirits can have their attention focused elsewhere. Sometimes, it is because they feel like their communication will not serve a higher purpose, or that it is unnecessary at that particular time.

As for the question of whom they communicate through, that is a different matter. Remember that it is easier for spirits to connect with those of a higher vibration, so they will come to people who can see and feel and hear and know them more easily so that they don't have to lower their vibration any more in order to communicate with a physical person. If someone is contacted frequently with messages from the other side, it means they offer less resistance and are functioning at a higher vibration. This is often why deceased loved ones come during the dream state—our vibration is high and we lack resistance at that time.

In any case, your communication with the spirit world continues to grow and evolve as you continue to practice and utilize some of these tools to facilitate your connection. As with any good communication, it is healthy to maintain boundaries that feel safe and comfortable to you, especially as you are first learning. It is not always easy to grasp a love connection that can extend beyond a physical lifetime. But, again, the more willing you are to expand your awareness and openness to these connections of the heart, the stronger you will experience—and validate—messages from your deceased loved ones as you both continue your spiritual growth.

11

Mastering the Language of Love

. . . .

All goes onward and outward, nothing collapses,
And to die is different from what any one supposed, and
luckier.
                    —Walt Whitman, "Song of Myself VI"

Mario was a nineteen-year-old, multitalented young man who
was full of life. This kid had a smile that would light up a room.
He also had a very rare and aggressive form of cancer called
alveolar soft part sarcoma, or ASPS.

Mario was the nephew of one of my clients, and when his
family called to ask if I would do Reiki on him, I said absolutely.
He had recently been diagnosed with ASPS, and he was in a
tremendous amount of pain. At the time of their call, Mario
had already gone through chemotherapy only to discover
that ASPS is a chemo-resistant cancer and there is currently
no known cure. He had been receiving pain medication consistently, but it was no longer working. They were looking for
alternative ways to relieve his suffering.

Because Mario was so weak and sick, I would have to go
to his house, which I typically don't do because my schedule

doesn't allow it. However, this was clearly a special case, and Spirit said go, so I did.

Once I arrived at Mario's house, I was greeted with a unique situation. Mario's parents were divorced and both had remarried. However, both parents had agreed to come back together to support their son and his journey. Their willingness to look past their differences was a beautiful expression of love.

But I could also feel desperation and fear in the house. Mario's parents understandably wanted to ease his pain and cure his cancer. They had heard Reiki might help, and I explained that Reiki is an ancient Japanese technique for stress reduction and relaxation that also promotes healing. I shared with them how it is administered by a "laying on of hands," and that it is based on the idea that an unseen life-force flows through us and is what causes us to be alive. If one's life-force is low, then we are more likely to get sick or feel stress. If it is high, we are more capable of being happy and healthy. I would work with Mario as a channel, letting that energy flow through me in whatever way was for his highest good. Mario's family seemed open to the idea, so I began a Reiki session with Mario's parents watching protectively over us.

To start, I had Mario sit in a comfortable chair, and we talked a bit just so I could get to know him better. He was very uncomfortable physically and had a lot of pain in his neck and back. The tumor had started in his hip, so there was a tremendous amount of pain throughout his hip and spine as well. Once the hour was over, Mario said he did feel some relief. I talked with his parents for a bit and indicated that if they noticed that it was helping him, I would be happy to come back to the home another day.

Two days later, Mario's father called and asked me to come back. The Reiki seemed to have taken his pain away. He said,

"We don't necessarily understand what you are doing, but whatever it is, it is working for him. If you would come back that would be great." And so I did.

I went back again and again. I would do Reiki, and we would talk about what was going on with him and how he was feeling—not just physically, but mentally, emotionally, and spiritually as well. I saw Mario about once a week, and we got to know each other very well. We had some great talks. I learned that my friend Mario was a musician (he was in a band) and was very athletic (he'd started on the varsity football team before his illness). He was quite popular and an all-around great guy. I could tell that everyone loved Mario.

He also shared with me that in his senior year of high school, he'd discovered a bump on his hip and went to the doctor. Shortly thereafter they received the diagnosis of cancer. He said that they walked him through what the treatment plan would be, and he went into it with high hopes, truly believing that he would be cured. As he shared his story, I could feel that his beliefs had changed. He was losing hope.

I continued to see Mario every week, sometimes twice a week. Each time I visited him, I saw him getting weaker and weaker physically, mentally, and emotionally. It broke my heart, and one day I just had to talk with him about it. So I said, "You've had a different energy the past couple weeks, Mario. I really feel the need to ask you what you are feeling. What are you going through? What's happening *within* you?"

At that point he broke down and started to cry. He didn't have any words, but I could tell he wanted to share. So I asked him a question that can be very difficult but is also so important: "Are you tired of fighting? Because if you are tired, Mario, it is OK."

Mario felt there was a lot of pressure on him to get better, and he too wanted to get better. But he was getting so tired. He didn't want to let anyone down, and he felt he needed to fight to stay alive for his parents. They wanted him to be here. He was very close to his brother as well, and he wanted to be there for him too. I told Mario that if he was ready to go, his family would be OK. I told him they would not want him to continue to suffer. This was a very hard conversation to have, especially with a nineteen-year-old, but it needed to happen.

Thinking about a nineteen-year-old dying because cancer is ravaging his body is heartbreaking. He still had his whole life to live. But Mario was in so much pain he couldn't live that life. He told me he didn't want to take the medication anymore. It just made him feel worse. In his parents' eyes, the medication was offering hope, but in Mario's eyes, it was his death sentence.

I held Mario's face in my hands and looked him right in the eyes and told him that he needed to be honest with himself and his parents. When he was ready to share how he really felt, and wanted support, I would be there to help him in whatever way I could. I assured him that his family was not going to be angry with him. They would feel sad, because from their point of view if he quit taking his medication then they would have to come to grips with his death. But his family would eventually understand, because every day they witnessed the pain and physical discomfort he was in was torture for them too.

What Mario truly wanted, at this point, was to live without the medication. He wanted some quality of life, which he felt he had given up in exchange for some quantity of life. I left him that day having witnessed the love he had for his family and knew deep inside that the love he had for himself would soon allow him to go home.

A couple days later he called me and asked me to come back sooner than our next scheduled appointment. His physical body was emaciated, but his spirit was shining. I could see that Mario had definitely come to a place where he was ready to go. He hadn't voiced that yet, but there was an unspoken knowing between us. We talked about the intimate conversations Mario had had with each family member and that he had asked his friends to come over one at a time. What Mario's friends didn't know was that he was preparing to say good-bye in his own way. I did ask him to come to me in spirit, when he could. We hugged. I kissed him on the forehead, and I left with my heart beating faster than normal. This kid had found a way into my heart, and as much as I didn't want to see him go, I knew it was time. I left that day knowing I would never see him again in physical form.

As I was driving home, I was trying to decide if I should let his parents know that he was getting close to transitioning. I could feel it. I asked Spirit to help me, and if I was meant to share, then I would be guided. Mario's father called me the next day. I took that as a sign, and so I told him, "Mario is getting ready to leave. I just feel like you should know that."

His dad said, "No, he is still fighting."

I replied, "He is fighting for you guys. He is not fighting for himself any longer. He has told me he is ready to go."

It was the hardest thing to say to a grieving father, and his response was one of absolute love.

"If that is the case, we will let him go. We don't want to see him in pain any longer."

It was a heartbreaking, heart-opening moment for both of us.

Later that day, Mario and his family had that honest conversation. And the next day he developed a fever. Four days later, he passed away.

Mario's funeral was the largest I have ever seen. More than 750 people attended. In the short time he was here, Mario had touched so many lives in ways he'd never even known. He lived life one day at a time and had accomplished so much at just nineteen. I believe that on a soul level Mario knew he would not live a long life here in the physical realm, but he sure lived a full one. He was a shining light in the lives of so many. Even in his passing, he was teaching others about love.

After the funeral I was told that during the four days he had the fever, he had each family member come in one by one to tell them how much he loved them. He made each of them make him a promise: that when he passed over and enough time had gone by where they were emotionally stronger, they would take one of my classes. He wanted to be able to communicate with them. He told them that although he didn't understand any of this spiritual stuff himself, he truly felt like the love between them would live on and continue to create opportunities to connect.

Each and every family member and friend kept their promise, and shortly after his death Mario came to me through written word. It was just over two months after his passing and I was preparing to visit his family for the first of their "promised" classes. This is the message I received from Mario that day.

10/18/04

Hello Everyone,

I am so excited to have you all here together learning through me about this new world that I am now a part of . . . It is beautiful here . . . no pain, no worries . . . I have the wind blowing when I want, the rain when I want, and any time I want to be near water it is a mere thought and it is here . . . Incredible . . .

SO excited that you have all kept your promise . . . you are starting to notice little signs . . . Unfortunately, I haven't been able to work a whole lot with you . . . I am still learning how this new world works, so to speak.

Thank you for all that you have done in my memory . . . it is very touching to see all the people that have united for different things . . . I am truly excited about the place you have created for me. It is very special, and when you go there you know I am there with you.

Dad, I am talking to you in all ways. Please listen to me . . . You feel me sometimes but doubt what has been felt. There is no need to doubt . . . I am fully present in your life . . . in everyone's life.

It is much easier to be able to get around without the extra load to carry. The lights in the truck are dimming . . . that is me. Pay attention to the little things . . . Get closer to Nate, he needs some extra help to learn how to express his feelings and not keep them all bottled in . . . skating is one thing, but this is talking and healing that I am talking about.

Tell Brett that I hear him . . . he talks to me often but also doubts that I am there. He is struggling with indecision . . . feeling he should be at a certain place at this time in his life . . . things are all in alignment with his soul journey and he questions himself and his worth too much. Tell him to follow his heart . . .

Mom, listen to me. Sometimes you need to feel the pain . . . let it out . . . try not to hold it all in so that you can make it better. It is good to cry and release that sadness . . . I know you miss me, and would trade places with me in a minute, but this is what I came there to do, to teach others how to live a true, loving life. There were times when I was so excited about my life, and couldn't believe my luck . . . it was like a dream. Now I know that it seems like all lives are just dreams . . . and then we are back home . . . to create a new "dream." It really is fun learning and growing . . .

Music is such a big part of life . . . keep listening . . . Let the joy in. Tell Evan to keep playing. He has a gift. Trust that there is a place in his life for it and he doesn't have to choose between one or the other . . . he knows what I mean. When you listen to him, think of me. I am there, singing right along with him . . . You will feel my spirit there, if you try.

Love to you all . . .

Thank you, Sunny, for being here to help as my family and I grow together . . . Until next time . . .

Mario

And Mario has kept his promise, too. His messages were validated by his family, and they carried them all through the pain and sadness into hope and love. Mario's family became aware not only through his death, but through messages like this afterward, that the love never ends.

The wisdom and grace of this young man came largely in his awareness that his death was only a beginning, and that his new journey required new tools and new ways to maintain that expression of love. He did not fully understand it. His family did not fully understand it. The purpose of a life ending so soon was certainly hard for me to grasp, as well.

There are many reasons someone would choose to stay on Earth longer than perhaps they should: out of regret, out of guilt, out of concern for those they will leave behind. But what we need to know in our hearts is that it is enough to love, enough to trust, enough to believe that the connection can—and will—live on. And by taking the steps to allow opportunities for this new mode of communication to nurture and grow is all that is necessary for that trust and belief to become a part of our reality. That connection remains strong and ongoing.

12
You Are Not Alone
in Your Grief

● ●

When you are born, you cry, and the world rejoices. When you die, you rejoice, and the world cries.

—Buddhist saying

In all my work with the spirits, they have usually reported back that they felt an intense sense of peace and love upon crossing over to the other side. They experience feelings that can't even be described in words but are sometimes communicated through colors unfamiliar to us in the physical world. I don't know if I would say they are experiencing something in the physical that makes it easier to let go, or whether moments before they leave they see and feel the energy of the spirit world which allows them to release their resistance. It's almost as though it is the body acknowledging its freedom. This peace is often the expression that is left for us to witness and hopefully carry with us when they pass on.

Sure, there is heartache, sadness, and loss for those who die. The smell of good food cooking in the kitchen, the sight of fresh flowers on an afternoon walk, the coos of babies, belly laughs with friends, jumping for joy, holding your partner—all of these things and many more will be missed. But I am told that all of these and more exist in the spirit world, just not in the same form. And although we feel like we would miss it because it is what we know right now, going home is so much better than we could ever imagine with our human mind. And, once there, we would not consider coming back except for the carrot of expansion and contrast dangling in front of us.

If the deceased desires to stay more connected to their loved ones, then they can tune into our frequency and feel our sadness. This is often the case when they first transition and are still in a healing space. Once they have transcended that area, then it is likely that they would not feel sadness or pain, just love.

If a spirit is in a healing space, they work on forgiveness and releasing the pain and sadness they still carry. They also heal from the pain they caused others in that life. Not everyone needs to go to a healing space (and I don't know how this is decided). At that point, the awareness of how nothing was ever actually wrong infuses the spirit, and all is well.

Your loved ones are with you throughout the grieving process, from the funeral and beyond. They aren't in their body any longer, they are in spirit, but they are nonetheless present alongside you. In fact, we're all already in spirit, in a way; it is simply embodied for us right now. Meaning, your spirit enters your body when you are born, and when your body dies, your spirit leaves your body to go back home. Everyone is a spirit and follows this same journey. As I write this, this quote by Pierre Teilhard de Chardin comes to mind: "We are not human beings having a spiritual experience; we are spiritual beings having a human experience."

Many African and other traditional tribal cultures are accustomed to communication without words or touch. Some have even been known to communicate telepathically over many miles. In groups, they often speak very little, as their more direct means of communication is beyond words. It is heart-to-heart—a practice that is learned early and continues throughout their whole life.

In these tribes, it is believed that when an elder passes, they become a member of the ancestral elders who guide the tribe. Because of their tradition of heart-to-heart communication, there is no loss when the elder passes. The communication that they have enjoyed for a lifetime is still available with the now-ancestor, who will continue to guide the tribe from the higher realms. The elder becomes one of the spiritual helpers for the tribe, and the tribe knows that they can contact them by raising their vibrations; thus, they know that they have not actually "lost" the strength and love of their elder.

Grief is a natural response to the loss of someone you love dearly. But oftentimes our grief gets in the way of feeling love. Instead, all that is felt is sadness and loss. It is this sadness and loss that we hold on to, which then blocks the love and the connection to our loved ones from the spirit world. If you are grieving, please remember this: You cannot focus on the absence of your loved ones and find the presence of them. Continuing your relationship requires a letting go on your part, which we'll work through in this chapter.

Grief is a very personal thing, and in my experience no two people grieve in the same way. Everyone walks the journey of loss individually. Many grief specialists say that you will go through specific phases: denial and isolation, anger, bargaining, depression, and finally acceptance. I have never liked any sort of blanket statement for such a personal emotional process like this because people frequently try to identify where they are in the process and if they are "normal" or not. I feel this halts the grieving process and does not honor their spiritual guidance and heart connection to their loved ones.

Although I don't necessarily agree with the traditional approach completely, I do think it is important to address what is out there on the subject of grief. I'd like to cover both ends of the grief philosophy. Know that whichever ideas resonate with you are perfect for you for now . . . and you may even find your own truth elsewhere. To start, let's explore grief from the traditional standpoint.

The Five Traditional Stages of Grief

The five traditional stages of grief were first proposed by Elisabeth Kübler-Ross in her 1969 book *On Death and Dying*. She says that in our bereavement, we spend different lengths of time working through each step:

1. Denial and isolation
2. Anger
3. Bargaining
4. Depression
5. Acceptance

And we express each stage more or less intensely. The five stages do not necessarily occur in order, and we can often move between stages before achieving a more peaceful acceptance of death. Many of us are not afforded the luxury of time required to achieve the final stage of grief, acceptance.

The death of a loved one might inspire you to evaluate your own feelings of mortality. Throughout each stage, a common thread of hope emerges: *As long as there is life, there is hope. As long as there is hope, there is life.*

Many people do not experience the stages in the order listed above, and this is OK. The key to understanding the stages is not to feel like you must go through every one of them, in precise order. Instead, it's more helpful to look at them as guides in the grieving process—it helps you understand and gain context for where you are.

A New Way to Grieve

"Loss is forever, but grief is not." What if this statement were true? What if we began to look at loss as a forever, in the sense that the physical body is lost? Loss is something that happens to everyone at some point in their lives in a variety of ways, death included. Grief, however, is not forever; and it certainly is not an absolute. It is time to see death, grief, and loss through the eyes of love. Love lives on, forever, in the souls of those we love. It cannot end. It never ends.

The Tao of Grief

My friend and colleague Peter Hill wrote a chapter in his book *Warrior Work* called "The Tao of Grief," and his words were pure truth to my soul. I couldn't have said it any better myself.

In Peter's words,

Grief is a powerful energy and the word itself traces back to an old French word meaning deep sorrow; but that in turn goes back to an older Latin word meaning to push or press down. Everyone at some point in their life gets to feel the flow of grief pressing, pushing and spinning its way through their being. It can come like a tsunami, flooding the brain with waves of colors and sounds that dissolve the outer world until it passes and leaves the world forever changed. It may feel like a huge block of stone crushing down on you, leaving you breathless and paralyzed. Grief can impact you like a waterfall or a rain shower of tears that expands the heart's cavity until only emptiness and numbness remain. It can spread through your body like a firestorm, the heat making you weak in your knees, short of breath and the feeling of the heat expanding your being beyond the boundaries of your body. You might even feel its energy like a vise, squeezing your heart, making you faint and trembling in shock. Whatever form it takes, the Tao of Grief is to shatter the Maya, the illusion that is form, and to be a sharp reminder of the short time we have to navigate the roles and worlds of our life here in this space and time. It puts us in touch with our energetic core and, within that core, the INTENT we come out with will shape the next three months to five years of our life.

The time shortly after grief impacts one's being is a crucial window of intention. People who do not want to live after a loved one leaves often follow within a short time. People who have repressed their gifts and buried goals will embark on new paths, new careers and new relationships that are uncovered by the fire of grief. Others may draw darkness and despair into their lives by building armor around their hearts and walls around their soul to try and keep the grief at bay—to keep from feeling it ravage their being and destroying their illusion of control.

You may not be able to choose when grief comes into your path, but you can choose how you embrace it. Let it flow through your being. Listen to the lessons it brings; express it (mourn) through writing, singing, collages, art, movement, sharing their life story with others, quiet reflection or other ways that speak to you. From it, you will be transformed into a brighter and clearer being of light with dignity, purpose and direction. And in that space you will realize that we can never truly lose anyone, nor can they lose us. They are woven into the fabric of our being as we are woven into theirs. It will also help you to enjoy and appreciate your form and theirs, and have true gratitude for the time and space you share. Grief will have broken the shell that enclosed you and opened your eyes and heart and being to new realities and worlds that were hidden, but always right in front of you.[2]

In my life I have lost many loved ones, clients, and friends, and I have walked the journey of loss and grief. I have grown through every single death in my life even though initially I felt heartbreak and loss. Each death has touched my soul in a different way. As I've grown in my awareness, I've been able to really see the blessings in death, to see death through the eyes of love. As a medium, I have also communicated with spirits who have tried desperately to put us at ease, to let us know that they are OK, they are not in pain, and they are still with us. Their message almost always is: I love you and will always be with you.

Grief can hold you back from receiving the message of love or even seeing or feeling your loved ones around. It can cause such deep pain and sadness that you can't hear or see the signs that a medium might be able to see. That is why I do the work I do. Ultimately, I believe that everyone can connect with their loved ones on their own. However, especially at times when the pain is so strong, a medium can connect the physical and spirit worlds together more easily because they are not personally involved. They are able to raise their vibration and tune into the energy easier because it is not their own personal experience, so they can be objective.

If you want to be able to connect with your loved ones on a deeper level, then you must move through your grief. The

---

2   Peter Hill, "The Tao of Grief," *Intent Blog* (December 28, 2008): http:// intentblog.com/tao-grief. Reprinted courtesy of Peter Hill.

following exercise is one way to release some of that pain to allow the healing to occur.

The Four Tasks of Mourning

J. William Worden, PhD, professor of psychology at Harvard Medical School, developed an approach to grieving that he calls the Four Tasks of Mourning. Loss and grief are part of life, but this model suggests that there is much we can do to successfully complete the work of mourning. Worden's grief work can be summarized by the acronym TEAR:

T = To accept the reality of the loss

E = Experience the pain of grief

A = Adjust to a world without the deceased

R = Reinvest emotional energy in another relationship

To Accept the Reality of the Loss

When someone dies, even if the death is expected, there is a sense that it hasn't happened. The first task of grieving is to face the reality that the person is dead, that the person is gone and will not return, that reunion in this life is impossible. Denying the facts of the loss, the meaning of the loss, or the irreversibility of the loss only serves to prolong the grief process. Though denial or hope for reunion is normal immediately after the loss, this illusion is usually short-lived.

Experience the Pain of Grief

Many people try to avoid the painful feelings in various ways, such as by "being strong," moving away, avoiding painful thoughts, or "keeping busy." There is no adaptive way of avoiding grief. You must allow yourself to experience and express your feelings. Anger, guilt, loneliness, anxiety, and depression are among the feelings and experiences that are normal during this time. Recall and relate both pleasant and unpleasant memories of the deceased. Ask for the support of friends. Tell them what you need from them, because people often misunderstand the needs of those grieving. Be assured that the memory of your loved one will continue, but the pain will lessen in time and will eventually disappear.

Adjust to a World Without the Deceased

Many survivors, especially widowed persons, resent or fear having to develop new skills and take on roles that were formerly performed by the deceased. There may be many practical daily affairs you need help with and advice on, but there will be a great sense of pride in being able to master these challenges. The emotions involved in letting go are painful but necessary to experience. If you don't adapt and change, you will remain stuck in the grief process and unable to resolve your loss.

Reinvest Emotional Energy in Another Relationship

The final task is to affect an emotional withdrawal from the deceased person so that this emotional energy can be used in continuing a productive life. This does not necessarily mean finding a new spouse, surrogate mother, or best friend. It does mean reentering the stream of life without your deceased loved one. You must rebuild your own ways of satisfying your social, emotional, and practical needs by developing new or changed activities or relationships. This is *not* dishonoring the memory of the deceased, and it doesn't mean that you love him or her any less. It simply recognizes that there are other people and things to be loved, and you are capable of loving.[3]

The Four Tasks of Mourning begin when the honeymoon period is over, after the friends have stopped calling, after everyone thinks you should be over it, after the court case is resolved. "Closure" has been effected, and everything is supposed to be back to normal. It's at this point that the real grieving begins. Notice that the first step of Worden's grief work is *acceptance*, which is the last stage of the five stages of grief.

Listen to your spirit. It will guide you to the best way for you to work through your grief and mourning . . . if you will listen. There is no one right way; however, it is important that you find *a* way. If you want to communicate with your loved ones who have passed, it is much easier to do so when your vibration is higher. Carrying the heaviness of grief keeps you dense, lowering your vibration. Moving through your grief allows you to feel the love connection and to see, feel, hear, and know the presence of your loved ones right beside you, loving you through it all.

Love is everywhere . . . even in death. Love spreads as the calls come in and the news is shared. Love brings together far-flung families and friends. Love is compassion in action, for the days, weeks, and months that follow a loss. However, you have to have your eyes open to see it—and this can be difficult to do when we are hurting.

The depth of the pain we feel when we lose someone is equal to the depth of love we have to gain from the experience.

---

3   J. William Worden, "Four Tasks of Mourning," in *Grief Counseling and Grief Therapy: A Handbook for the Mental Health Practitioner, Third Edition* (New York: Spring Publishing, 2009).

Notice that I didn't say the depth of love we had for the person we lost. I said the depth of love we have to gain. Death *expands* us. It allows us to grow in ways we never knew, and likely never wanted to. When denied, death offers grief, pain, loss, anger, and sadness. When embraced, it can offer all of those things as well, momentarily. However, when death is truly embraced, it can offer you a connection that is greater than time and space. A relationship like you never knew. A love that never dies, but simply changes form.

As a psychic medium, I have been blessed to be a support to people, both living and deceased, in connecting with their loved ones. It has been an absolute gift for me, as it has taught me time and time again that love never ends. It only changes form. There was a time in my life when I didn't believe that. And, the interesting thing is that it wasn't death that taught me. It was love.

13
Being a Messenger of Love

• •

And now abide faith, hope, love, these three; but the greatest of these is love.

—1 Corinthians 13

My grandmother began showing signs of Alzheimer's about four years before she died. The diagnosis of the disease was not a surprise, as the signs had been there for years. However, it was certainly a challenge to find the purpose of this particular disease, as it seems so devastating from almost every point of view. At the very least, it creates a situation where physically communicating with love becomes difficult for everyone involved.

Once she was formally diagnosed, my independent grandmother understood that her safety was becoming an issue, so she left her home and moved in with her daughters. It was a tough thing for her to do, and she was, as one would guess, not happy about it. I remember her telling my mom after her house was sold that she no longer had a home—a common feeling amongst those who are moving between self-care and assisted living. My mom assured my grandma that their homes were now hers, but I know how hard it was on Grandma to give up her autonomy.

Having five daughters to depend on was certainly a relief for my grandmother after my grandpa died, but giving up her independence was hard. Within a year or so after his death, the disease had progressed to a point where it was impossible for my mother and her sisters to give my grandmother the quality of care she needed. They also found it increasingly difficult to keep track of her. She was a wanderer. She just could not sit still for a moment, and safety had become a pressing issue.

My mother and aunts made the decision to place Grandma in an assisted living center where she would get the twenty-four-hour care that she needed, and they ultimately chose a facility with a secure Alzheimer's wing in Tucson, where my mother lived. The weather was beautiful in Arizona over the winter months, and my grandmother really loved the environment. My mom would visit her daily, facilitating activities for everyone. They would sing, play games, and do little brainteasers. It was a heart-opening and heartbreaking experience, all at the same time. Even though Alzheimer's can be a devastating disease, I knew that I wanted to see it through the eyes of love.

In many ways Alzheimer's let me know my grandma on a deeper level. She was more present and in the moment than I had ever known her to be. You see, my grandma was an alcoholic my entire life, and most of her life as well, and Alzheimer's caused her to forget that, so she no longer drank. These moments of clarity were precious—for her and for us. It was especially cool to get to see her so often because the previous ten years we had lived farther apart.

During these visits I felt like we got to spend a lot of good, quality time together. I had two younger children at that time, so my sons, my mom, Grandma, and I would all sing nursery rhymes, eat ice cream, and just laugh and play. It was a very special time together—the moments I miss the most!

Then spring came, the weather got warmer, and the decision was made for Grandma to be in a cooler climate, where she could be outside more. The Arizona summers are extremely hot, and we were all concerned about it being too hot for her to be outside. So she moved back to Utah, where she was originally from and where the majority of the family lived. They chose a new assisted living center with a secure Alzheimer's wing, and she moved in April 2000. She lived there for eight months.

December 31, 2000, began like a pretty normal day. I woke up around 6:00 a.m. and made breakfast for my family. Christmas had just passed, it was New Year's Eve, and my brother had come to visit for a few days. We were all in the kitchen talking about the night's plans to celebrate the "real" millennium. This year, we had decided to actually go out and have some fun instead of falling asleep watching the ball drop.

I was excited to participate in the festivities, but this heavy feeling kept creeping in. I tried to ignore it, thinking it was just my fear of leaving my kids home with the babysitter or inevitably facing drunk drivers on the road later that night. As hard as I tried, that feeling just wouldn't go away. Something was wrong.

I finally told my family that I wasn't sure I wanted to go out. Something just didn't feel right. Then the phone rang, and our lives changed forever.

My mother was calling, or at least that is what the caller ID said. It didn't sound like her. She was crying hysterically, and I couldn't make out any of the words except "Grandma is dead." I tried to get my mom to calm down, as I truly could not understand what she was saying or why she was so upset. We had talked about Grandma dying several times and knew that once she did, she would be free from this terrible disease. In many ways, we thought it would be a relief when she finally did pass. So why was my mother screaming uncontrollably? Well, after several minutes I found out why. My grandmother hadn't died from Alzheimer's disease—she had died of hypothermia.

Over the course of the next few days and weeks, we pieced together the last few hours of Grandma's life. To the best of our knowledge, Grandma walked out of her "secure" Alzheimer's wing and out two other sets of doors in the middle of the night without anyone noticing her. Then she walked six-tenths of a mile in zero-degree weather with bare feet wearing only a silk nightgown. Her body was found twenty feet from the doorstep of someone's home.

We were all devastated to hear the horrific details of her passing. There were so many questions: How had this happened in a seemingly secure environment? How had no one seen her walking for that distance? Why did she have to suffer such a painful death, when we'd tried so hard to protect her?

I also questioned the why, but soon my attention turned to a different question: What could the purpose of this tragedy be? My heart truly felt that there was a bigger picture to this story; I just didn't understand it yet. I needed to move to a higher vibration in order to see the higher vision, but at that time I simply wasn't there yet.

Soon I would receive my answer. My love for my grandmother allowed me to remain open to her messages, and several days after her death she came to me in spirit form. Her presence was as clear to me as my hands are right now on my keyboard. She asked me—no, begged me—to be her voice. As I mentioned earlier, my grandmother was an alcoholic most of her life, and because she was not able to be present, she never truly felt like she was living her purpose, let alone knew what it was. But now, in death, she did: Her tragic ending would be the emotional voice and conduit that would bring about change.

It was in that brief but very powerful visit that I began to understand the bigger picture. Not only was I to fulfill this as my purpose, but I was to complete my grandmother's as well. My grandmother wanted me to speak up for those patients who could not. People needed to know about the care facilities and their lack of focused attention, the ratio of caregivers to patients, and their disregard for proper training. In many cases, elder care living facilities are not managed well. I wanted to help educate people about the laws governing care facilities, or the lack thereof, and what really took place behind the scenes.

I chose to honor Grandma by speaking to the media about the conditions that needed to be changed. I could no longer turn a blind eye to the elder care in our nation, and I didn't want anyone else to, either. My family and I asked a lot of questions—we interviewed patients and caregivers and then shared our story with newspapers and magazines.

As we kept the conversation going, more people began to listen. Our governor shared Grandma's story, and there was enough interest that three of us flew out to Washington, DC to attend Senate hearings on public policy and talk with our senators. Most people's first response was empathy for the tragic way in which Grandma had died. That empathy inspired them to genuinely want to see change. It was an amazing experience.

After my trip to DC, I became a board member of the Alzheimer's Association and a supporter of the Safe Return program, which provides twenty-four-hour nationwide emergency response service for individuals with Alzheimer's. In our sharing my grandmother's story, we helped save lives. Our voices created public awareness that effectively changed local laws. My grandmother was now the unspoken hero in the lives of many Alzheimer's patients who would now have better quality care, safer physical environments, and caregivers who were held to a higher standard.

My ability to understand this new language of love from the other side allowed me to take guided action and use my voice. I could provide the outlet for my grandmother to be heard and then share her inspiration and guidance that would ultimately have a positive effect on many, many other people. Together, we had made a difference.

Through this experience, I learned what it meant to be authentic and to own my power. I understood for the first time that it was time to stop playing it safe. Up to this point, I was a stay-at-home mom and was quite happy doing that. But after my grandmother's death, something within me changed. The voice, the student and the teacher, awoke in me. I was now ready to consciously live my purpose through teaching, speaking, and sharing. My grandma's death was the catalyst for me to release my fears and to put myself out there. I embraced my inner calling: to love myself enough to be who I really am; to acknowledge the messages I was receiving from all realms; and to confidently use my voice and share those messages with others.

Grandma's story does not end here. The love continues. I tell her story quite often in my workshops and speaking engagements. She has been a beautiful teacher and guide to me throughout the years, and I stand in unending appreciation of all we have learned together.

Owning and Speaking Your Truth

I have discovered over the years, through my own personal experiences and through witnessing others, how difficult yet powerful it is to step into your truth. Oftentimes the reason people struggle with stepping into their truth is because they are afraid of being judged, rejected, or even persecuted. What I have learned is that now is the time to stand in your power. You can do this through love and light and peace. You can be the change you wish to see by using your voice to speak your truth.

One of the greatest disservices we can do to others and ourselves is to not honor our own truth. Now, this doesn't mean throwing your truth in someone's face without regard for person, place, or timing; it does mean being authentic and not hiding your true self for fear of not being who others want you to be. This is easier said than done, and it actually takes a lot of effort to do. I see my clients struggle, as I have, to live their truth time and time again.

For example, a client will come in for a reading and say, "So, do you think I am crazy for thinking my deceased son is sitting in the passenger seat when I drive at night?" I tell them, "*No*, I don't think you are crazy. If you're crazy, then I am crazy too, because he is actually standing right beside you telling me about it now." The client, however, continues to express conflict within. She truly believes her son is visiting her (which he is), but her family or friends don't. They think she has gone off the deep end. Maybe she needs medication, or her grief is so deep she is imagining things. People fear what they don't understand; but that doesn't mean you have to shut down your intuition and not own your truth.

Speaking your truth can be as simple as saying, "I appreciate your concern and I love you dearly, but I believe the way I believe, and it brings me peace of mind." You get to believe

how you believe. *The end.* No more explanations or justifica-
tions. If you don't have the ability or are too scared to speak up,
you could write a letter to the person or people that you feel
you lose your power to. You can say whatever it is you need to
say in the letter, and therefore own your power on the piece or
pieces of paper. I then suggest my clients burn the letter and
release it to the Universe, so as to send it to the higher dimen-
sion. Letter writing can be a great way to get more comfortable with your truth, and eventually you will find a way to share
these feelings with those involved when the time is right.

I was taught the word *satnam* when I was a child. My mom
told me that it meant "your truth is your truth and my truth is
my truth." She suggested I say it to myself when I felt like I was
being picked on for my beliefs or felt like an outsider. I said
this often to myself, and the word would help me feel a little
more powerful each time.

Speaking your truth, listening to your heart, and loving
yourself—regardless of whether people believe in what you
believe in or not—are fabulous ways to raise your vibration and
keep you connected to the spirit world. When you hold your
truth within, your vibration becomes dense and is oftentimes
disguised as blame. Blame typically happens when you don't
speak up, and you hold the person that "wouldn't allow you to
speak your truth" responsible. In reality, it was you all along.
Blame makes you sick physically and mentally, and ultimately,
it takes your power away.

Be mindful to recognize the difference, however, between
your truth and your opinions. Opinions want to be right and
are usually based on ego and judgment. Truth, on the other
hand, comes from a deep sense of authenticity and vulner-
ability. Truth is what is real for us on a *soul level.* I find that
especially with this topic, life after death, it is so important to

honor your personal truth as well as others'. It can ultimately be what helps you connect with the spirit world on an even greater level. And remember, if others don't believe, don't take it personally. They just haven't had the experience, that's all. It is all in divine time. *Satnam!*

Epilogue

The Love Never Ends

Messages from the other side are our gifts from the spirit world. When we connect, receive, and acknowledge the message, that is our gift back to them. These special messages remind us that our loved ones continue to watch over us. Through interacting with us, they can reveal guidance and information that may only make sense through their eyes, since they can see through the eyes of love. Remaining open to them gives us the opportunity to do that as well, if we are willing to learn.

Once in spirit, our deceased loved ones see with clarity. There is no judgment or pain because their higher vibration and perspective take the pain away. Things just are. There is no right or wrong. Life can and does continue, but it is our choice about how we continue on . . . in pain, grief, anger, and sadness or in healing, learning, growing, expanding, and loving.

Maintaining a connection with our loved ones after their death can actually inspire us. It can cause us to wake up with joy in our hearts, to embrace life more fully, not push against it with fear. We have an opportunity to live with the awareness that life continues beyond our physical existence. There is not a separation until you create it with fear of the unknown.

My relationships with those who have passed have taught me so much personally: Welcome the life you have yet to live, and appreciate every moment of every day. See and feel how important it is to be present in each and every one of those memories. Love yourself and each other, without condition. Forgive yourself and one another by realizing that there truly is nothing to forgive.

We have all cast the perfect characters for our life experiences. Those who have filled an important role in our lives are playing the part that we ourselves called forth, so as to learn even more about love. Remember that even the uncomfortable experiences in life teach. They may have taught you what you didn't want, which still provides evidence and clarity for what you *do* want . . . and gets you closer to it. That is a tremendous gift.

And our learning doesn't end there. The spirit world is a mental world, so after this life our thoughts will create our afterlife experiences. Once there, you will continue to learn and grow, creating new experiences beyond what you ever imagined in the physical world.

We are reminded by Spirit every day that we are love and are loved. We are loving beings in a physical world that are connected to an afterlife that does indeed exist. (I have never been able to get an address to where the afterlife resides, per se, but it is everywhere. It's in the stars and walking alongside us. It's literally everywhere.) We have all around us this amazing team of deceased loved ones, spirit guides, angels, archangels, ascended masters, and the Divine. They are just waiting for us to ask for help, to allow them in, to truly hear them. They are standing beside you right now. Can you feel them? They are the whisper in your ear, the chills down your spine. They are the presence beside you and the vision in your mind. They are ready to begin this new and expanded journey. Are you?

It is possible to let go of fear and realize that it is only an illusion of great power that prevents us from fully living. Everyone dies, but not everyone really lives. Communicating with the spirit world will allow your soul to open up. You will feel connected, guided, and even exhilarated.

You will begin to understand that everything here on Earth is imperfectly perfect. You will know that your loved ones in spirit see what is invisible to your eyes. You will recognize that everything is in perfect divine order. Everything, including death, is in perfect order.

Spirit is always communicating with us in all its forms, not just through our deceased loved ones. You have access to communication with angels and archangels, spirit guides, ascended masters, and many other light beings. All you have to do is stay connected with them by inviting them into your life. Open yourself up to their guidance and communication through meditation. Stay present in your physical world. Look for the signs from Spirit. They are everywhere. If you keep communicating with your guides, they will absolutely continue communicating with you. The truth is, they will actually try to communicate with you even if you don't do anything . . . but the problem with that is, you probably wouldn't notice.

If you will connect with them long enough, you might even realize that there is no real moral code in the spirit world. By letting go of the judgment of right and wrong, this awareness could create more freedom than you have ever experienced. You don't have to wait to die to feel freedom! You don't have to wait to die to feel absolute, unconditional love. Love is who you are and what you are made of. You don't have to wait until you die to feel and know these things . . . but you can. The choice is up to you. It is OK to wait, but why wait? Why not embrace it all now? Either way, your loved ones will be there, waiting for you and loving you all the way!

So, are you ready to live your life for this moment? Are you ready to pay tribute to your deceased loved ones by living full out? And by full out, I mean loving, every step of the way. Not hiding behind fear any longer, but instead standing up and stepping into the unknown. You are Spirit embodied. You have the knowledge. You have the connection. You have the love. You have your loved ones waiting for you. What more do you need? A little push? You got it. Ready or not, let's do it. Let's jump in and create the life you truly desire: a life of love and joy and connection. Let's live from a place of love. Let's be willing to ask for and receive help from the spirit world. It starts today! Are you in? Yes!

I'll see you there . . . where the love never ends!

Sunny Dawn Johnston

Acknowledgments

I stand in unending appreciation of all of those who have walked before me and paved the way, of those who walk beside me and hold my hand every day, and of those who will walk after me and expand the beauty of life in their own unique way.

There are not enough words to express all the gratitude and love I have in my heart, nor is there enough time to mention every person whom I hold near and dear. Let's suffice it to say that I am honored, blessed, and humbled to walk this journey. Without the love in my heart, it would all be meaningless. Therefore, I begin my appreciation with the nameless, the Oneness, the Divine, Spirit, the God of my understanding. The support from the nonphysical realm, especially in the writing of this book, has been remarkable. I intend to expand my connection to even greater depths of love and continue the journey as an extraordinary student of life.

My infinite appreciation and heartfelt gratitude go to the following people:

My mom and dad, who taught me my first lessons about love and life. You have been the perfect guides for my soul's unique journey.

My brothers, whom I continue to love, learn from, and grow with every day.

My children, whose love, humor, support, and independence continually teach me how to love, laugh, and lighten up. I am in awe of the amazing men you have become. You are my light!

My husband, who has stood beside me since the minute we met. Your unconditional love, acceptance, patience, and support have given me the opportunity to be who I am and do what I do.

My Sunlight team, who support me in any and all ways. Without your time, energy, and support this book would not have been written. I am so blessed to have a group of women who "get" me and the way I work.

My students and clients, you inspire me to expand and grow every day. You call me to listen and to be present. I am honored that you have invited me into your life.

My readers, who I believe called this book into form. Without your interest, intent, and desire this book may have stayed within me for years.

An extra special thank-you to those families whose stories I share in this book. May the loss of your loved one serve as a blessing in the lives of those who read this. May they experience, through your stories, a new way of seeing not only death, but life! May your journey help them realize that the love never ends!

Appendix

Common Questions about Death and the Afterlife

Can you tell when someone is going to pass, even if they aren't sick?

There are some mediums who tune into that more than others. I have had experiences when I have felt that, for some unknown reason, but it is not common for me.

I lost my amazing dad at 12:02 a.m., and three days later at 12:05 a.m. my beautiful mum suffered a massive stroke and died as well. Bearing in mind she had Alzheimer's and didn't even know Dad was ill, do you believe my dad went to get my mum?

The disease of the body is lifted once we pass over, so Alzheimer's would not affect her spirit as it transcended this physical Earth. Yes, I would believe that your father would be there to receive your mom, even though he had only passed over a few days earlier. Remember, the spirit is no longer in a body. The spirit world is mental, so as soon as he thinks about being with her, he can be, and he can be in more than one place at once as well.

When my grandma passed, it was a two-day process. During that time she talked about seeing an angel at the foot of her bed, my grandpa, who had gone ten years before her, as well as her siblings who had been gone a long time. Are those who went before really there waiting for us? We talk about "I will see you again when my time comes," but is it really true that we do see them again?

Yes, it is absolutely true that we see our deceased loved ones again. They are there to greet us once we transition and celebrate our birthday (the day of death in this physical world is a day of birth in spirit world), our homecoming.

Will I remember my life after I die?

Yes, you will remember your life—especially immediately after you pass. I am told, though, that everyone has different experiences and so there is not a one-size-fits-all answer. As you expand and grow, your memory becomes more distant. I can't say that your memories won't stay in part, but they will fade as your focus shifts in your new role. It's kind of like when you cram for a test and you remember everything for test day, and then the further away you get from the test, the less attention there is on it. It is not because it isn't important, but because you are now focused on something new. You can remember it, when something triggers it, but it isn't necessarily in your awareness any longer. Remember, we are trying to use human words and explanations for something that is not human, so the words won't always fit what they are trying to say, but it's the best way I can explain it.

Will I know everything I want to know after death?

In due time, but not all in an instant.

Will I see my loved ones again?!?

Absolutely. You will have the choice to connect with anyone you shared a heart connection with.

Will I know my family in heaven?

Yes, you will recognize them vibrationally, as everything is vibration first.

Will I get to see or feel my parents? How about my children?

Yes, if you choose to.

Will I see the ones who have passed before me? Will they be the age they were when they died? When my dad passed, he was fifty-one and I was twenty-five. Now I'm fifty-two. Will he know me?

Yes, you will see your deceased loved ones, though it is more like a feeling or knowing than literally seeing. The spirit world is a mental world. It is all thought-based, so you are recognizing their spirit based on their energy more than recognizing them based on their looks or age.

Will I miss my friends and family that I leave behind?

From what I hear, no. Not because you don't care, but because, when you transition, you are still with them if you desire to be.

So, how or why would you miss friends and family when they are right there with you?

If my deceased husband was married and widowed before marrying me, what will happen when I die? Is he with his first wife in heaven?

It is important to remember that when we return to the spirit world we are no longer in a body, so there is no physical limitation. And, love never ends. So, your husband can be with his first wife, or you, or both, based on desire. Looking at it from a human perspective, it seems as though we have to choose one partner or the other; but we do not have those limitations in the spirit world. There is no jealousy either, just love.

Will I be a part of the lives of those still living?

That is up to the individual spirit, but generally, yes. If there are things that are of interest to you happening in their lives, then you certainly would stay connected to them. Sometimes, as time goes on and people move through the healing process, it isn't as necessary. But if you want to, yes, you can.

Are you still able to visit and look after the ones you leave behind?

Yes, you absolutely can visit and look after your loved ones after you pass away. It is as easy as a thought.

Can spirits feel the emotions of their loved ones?

The spirit world connects with us through thoughts and feelings, so yes, they can tune into our emotions.

When I pass, will I be able to see my family, and will the same things that hurt me to see while I was here still hurt to see when I am gone?

My experience has been that the majority of the time, the spirits no longer care about material things. They are in a much higher vibration of love, so the things that once mattered no longer do. This is not all of the time, but most of the time.

Am I weird because I don't want to communicate with my dead loved ones?

No, many people are uninterested in communicating with their loved ones for a variety of reasons. It is OK if you don't want to. They won't take it personally.

When someone calls out a deceased person's name before they die, are they actually seeing that person?

Yes, typically the deceased loved one is there to welcome them to the other side. Remember that a death here is a birth there, and they are awaiting the birth.

How can I get concrete proof that anyone can communi cate with a loved one after they have passed?

The best way to get concrete proof is to have your own experience. Try opening yourself up to receiving a message from your loved one, or by going to a medium and allowing the loved ones to come through. During the reading you should hear things that validate that it is your loved one—that's your concrete proof. But most importantly, you should *feel* the truth of the message they are giving you throughout your body.

This part about reincarnation has always confused me: If my loved ones have moved on to another physical life, will they stop communicating with me?

I understand how it can be confusing. No, they do not stop communicating with us; that aspect of their soul still lives on. So, they can be reincarnated into another body, but they still retain all of the knowledge and information of the lives they have lived. Therefore, they can still communicate with you or a medium.

When someone commits suicide, does the person stay earthbound, or do they have the choice between staying earthbound and following the light?

I have seen both. Some have stayed earthbound; others have gone to the light right away.

Following a suicide, is the deceased's spirit trapped?

No, their spirit is not trapped. They are not any more trapped than any other spirit. Transitions offer freedom, not entrapment.

Will my deceased pets be waiting for me when I die?

This is a resounding YES!

I would ask you to sit down with my dog and figure out whose soul is in there. I swear he has human personality traits.

I have experienced when pets take on the energy of different loved ones, but they aren't actually a human soul. A human soul can impress the dog into doing things that might remind you of your loved one, but they do not "become" them.

What is the concept of time (or lack of time) in the spirit world?

Earth is but a speck of dust compared to the spirit world. The spirit world is an eternal world, transcending time and space.

What do the spirits of your parents do when you are having sex with your spouse?

The spirits watch. They aren't watching the bodies. There is no interest there, as they are not human. They watch the light show. Sex creates a kaleidoscope of color; it is a time when our energy is the most focused, the most magnificent, and they love the colors of our auras and the heart vibration that occurs.

Can I bypass friends and family and move up to hanging out with angels, saints, and Jesus and Mary? Is that the top level?

Well, I don't know about bypassing your friends and family, but can you evolve to a place of connecting with the angels and saints? Yes!

About the Author

SUNNY DAWN JOHNSTON is an internationally renowned psychic medium, teacher, author, and motivational speaker.

As a child, Sunny possessed innate wisdom, awareness, and curiosity of the angelic realm and spirit world. While she fought those gifts for many years, Spirit ultimately won, and Sunny began working full-time as a psychic medium in 2000.

Over the last fourteen years, Sunny has performed hundreds of readings for clients where she's communicated with spirits, guides, and their loved ones who have crossed over to the other side. The constant theme she receives from all of these divine entities and loved ones is this: Love never ends; fear exists only in this world.

In December 2003, Sunny founded Sunlight Alliance LLC, a spiritual teaching and healing center in Glendale, Arizona. Following her guidance, Sunny created a place where people could learn how to find and follow their personal spiritual path, recognize and own their natural spiritual gifts, and cultivate a spiritual connection with loved ones who have passed on. Sunny teaches her students that even in moments of adversity, we are not alone; our angels, guides, and loved ones who have crossed over are here to help us. Sunny's message of "love never ends" has drawn thousands of people from all over the world to her workshops, events, and private sessions.

Sunny is the best-selling author of *Invoking the Archangels, No Mistakes!, Living Your Purpose, A Wedding Officiant's Manual,* and *Find Me.*

Sunny speaks internationally on the subjects of angels, mediumship, and healing the heart. She has been featured on hundreds of local and national television and radio shows and has appeared in the award-winning documentary, *Sacred Journey of the Heart.* Her most recent endeavor has been starring in "A Séance with . . ." on Lifetime Movie Network.

Sunny is actively involved in the spiritual community and frequently conducts informational outreach work. She volunteers her time as a psychic investigator for the international organization Find Me. This is a not-for-profit association of Psychic, Investigative, and Canine Search & Rescue (SAR) volunteers working together to provide leads to law enforcement and families of missing persons and homicides. She lives in Glendale, Arizona with her family.

To learn more about Sunny's work, please visit her website www.sunnydawnjohnston.com and check out her Facebook page: SunnyDawnJohnstonFanPage.

Hier◯phantpublishing
books that inspire your body, mind, and spirit

Hierophant Publishing
8301 Broadway, Suite 219
San Antonio, TX 78209
888-800-4240

www.hierophantpublishing.com